I have known Dr. Carl Rafey for almost twenty years. He is a great chiropractor and also a close friend. Through my chiropractic work and consultation business, Aligned Performance, I have practiced many of the ideas that Dr. Rafey recommends. Very few people have taken the information he has with *Fix Your Stupid* and given an outline on how to reach your goals. Take the time to read this book and allow your life to be the best.

—Dr. Alok Trivedi, DC, behavior and peak performance expert

Carl Rafey, or "Doc," as I will always refer to him, is a very unique and forward-thinking man, who also happens to be a gifted chiropractor. I've worked with thousands of health-care professionals over the past twenty-five years, and very few have invested the time [it takes] to understand the dramatic effect a person's emotional health has upon their physical health or their life in general.

Fix Your Stupid will help each of us recognize when we are sabotaging ourselves and provide simple remedies to immediately put us back on the healthy track. Just like the best chiropractic care is preventive maintenance, Doc has created preventive maintenance in a handy guidebook for our personal emotional health.

—John Costino, corporate trainer and personal life coach

Fix Your Stupid is packed with valuable and helpful insights on how to get to the next level in your life. I encourage anyone wanting a healthy transformation to read this book.

—Dr. Carolyn Griffin, chiropractor, certified fermentationist, and founder of My Cultured Life

SMARTER THINKING FOR
A FAST CHANGING WORLD

Fix your Stupid

Live the Life you Deserve

FOREWORD BY STEVE SISGOLD

Dr. Carl Rafey, DC

FIX YOUR STUPID
LIVE THE LIFE YOU DESERVE

iUniverse books may be ordered through booksellers or by contacting:

iUniverse
1663 Liberty Drive
Bloomington, IN 47403
www.iuniverse.com
844-349-9409

ISBN: 978-1-6632-0247-5 (sc)
ISBN: 978-1-6632-0248-2 (hc)
ISBN: 978-1-6632-0246-8 (e)

Library of Congress Control Number: 2020914773

Print information available on the last page.

iUniverse rev. date: 09/09/2020

This book is dedicated to the person who always knows there is something better out there and searches for it: *you*—the you who has the determination to get the answers to go further in your life.

Some say seekers like us will never be happy or satisfied with life, but I have learned that being happy means you are always moving forward, expanding, and striving for more.

I dedicate this book to the *you* who wants and needs to keep growing and moving because that is what life is all about. I dedicate this book to *you*, and my dream is that what you receive from it plants a seed that will grow into a flower that blooms at just the right time, in the right situation, right when you need it. Just as one kernel of corn can create a corn stalk with many ears of corn and the ability to produce thousands of new stalks, you have the ability to create that type of expansion and exponential growth in your life. Here is to your abundance!

Always in your corner,
Carl

CONTENTS

FOREWORD

WHEN CARL FIRST TOLD ME THAT HE WAS WRITING A BOOK titled *Fix Your Stupid*, I felt a rush of energy up and down my spine. (By the way, that had nothing to do with his being a chiropractic physician.) It was the raw power of those three words that felt so real and captured the important message he wanted to convey in this book. Though the title is certainly provocative and maybe even offensive to some, what rang truest for me instantly was that I and many others do many unconscious things that we regret later. So why not just name it, and fix that stupid part of ourselves?

This book does exactly that; it shows you how to effectively catch your "stupid" thinking and change your thoughts and actions to more beneficial, "smart" strategies. He shares the results from doing that in a very reader-friendly and convincing manner. The success stories from him and his clients will also inspire you to get more focused and aware of your own thoughts and actions, plus ignite you and show you how to think smarter and succeed wildly and quickly.

Dr. Rafey has spent years studying, practicing, researching, and learning cutting-edge modalities from leaders in the fields of manifestation, spirituality, metaphysics, wellness, positive thinking, and self-motivation. I suggest you use what he shares, page by page, to the hilt! He also offers audio and video links to further help you get the best results possible from using his assessments and techniques.

Throughout the book, Dr. Rafey assures the reader that having "stupid thoughts" does not mean you are stupid—just the opposite. He shows us how to discover and catch these limiting thoughts, with no judgment, and see the gifts they teach us.

A spectacular read, a self-discovery course—*Fix Your Stupid* is a book that will face outward on my bookshelf to remind me that I always have the choice to focus my thoughts and actions and, therefore, as the book teaches, create my universe.

Enjoy the ride.

—Steve Sisgold
author, *Whole Body Intelligence*

ACKNOWLEDGMENTS

I WOULD LIKE TO THANK EVERYONE WHO PURCHASED THIS book or received it as a gift. In appreciation, I would like to offer you a free downloadable video program called "What You Must Do before You Take Any Action!" It's a perfect partner to the reading material in the pages that follow. Just go to www.fixyourstupid.com/bookgift and enjoy! *Great!*

Thank you also to my many life teachers for the courage and drive you displayed to get your work out there and share what you felt you had to share. Thank you for listening to your inner voices and following your guidance systems. Thank you for showing me how you always reach for more in your lives and how that serves you and others at the same time. Thank you for proving that true success and happiness come from serving others and being an inspiration to lift others up.

I also want to shine a bright spotlight on all the close friends I have made over the years in my chiropractic training program with Dr. Fred Schofield. When you know people well for a long time, you see the extreme aspects of life. I have watched and experienced great ups and downs over the years. I have learned not only from my experiences but also from spending time with many great people who have taken control of their lives and are now living the lives they dreamed of.

In turn, by spending this valuable time with people, I have also watched people spiral out of control when they could not stop thinking, talking, and focusing on what they didn't want. By doing so, they attracted more and more bad things into their lives. These lessons and examples have proven to me that you get what you think about, no matter if you want it or not.

This is a universe of attraction, not assertion. Nothing is forced on you. Anything that happens to you is because you have attracted it. That means you are powerful enough to change and create your life to make it the way you want it to be. The good life of health, wealth, love, and happiness can be yours too!

INTRODUCTION

I am excited to meet you in this way.

The book that you have in your hands is a culmination of all my life experiences and input from counselors, coaches, teachers, friends, family, and the hundreds of books that I have read.

In the moment that *Fix Your Stupid* was born, I committed to writing a book and began developing my system for shifting from the stupid mind to the smart mind. I am excited to share how to do that.

The one thing that always has left me in wonder is how so many people from so many walks of life, from such distant lands and different age ranges, can have the same ideas and messages at their cores, especially before the internet, blogs, podcasts, and other communication formats happened. My sense is that if you bought this book, then some of the ideas I write about may be things you have already thought about. I also would guess that a book called *Fix Your Stupid* either touched something inside you, intuitively, or brought up important questions you may have had, in terms of how to best create your desires in life. I want you to achieve your biggest goals! I want you to create your best life!

Throughout this book, I use the words *best life* to remind you that you have the choice to live your life in a smarter and more effective way—something I suspect you've already been considering, even if it was subconsciously. *Best life* is having high levels of and balanced health, wealth, and love. I'll give you a direct path for moving from your "stupid" self to your "smart" self—and how to do it quickly. By the way, one of my main daily objectives is to fix the stupid parts of myself, which you will read about as you turn these pages.

I will share tools and techniques and compelling stories of my own and of clients I have worked with over the years. This will keep you in your smart zone more so you can create better results in every area of your life. To reinforce my intention, at the end of each chapter, I include three affirmations and three questions.

I added specific affirmations that are specific truths of each chapter for you to repeat 108 times. "Why 108?" you might ask. There are several reasons: 108 is the number that many religions consider sacred. It is considered sacred because of the mathematical significance, so it is often used during religious ceremonies or during meditation, such as counting rosary or mala beads. In Hindu astrology, there are twelve signs of the zodiac and nine planets. Multiply 12 by 9 and you'll get 108. In regard to the chakras (intersections of energy lines in the body), there are said to be a total of 108 energy lines converging to form the heart chakra.

This is a number of huge importance throughout the world and throughout history, so reciting the affirmations at the end of each chapter 108 times reflects on that. Try it, and see how it works for you. It only takes a few minutes and will be worth every second.

The three questions at the end of the chapter are to stimulate you to apply what you have just learned to your life. My intention is for you to begin to fix your stupid right away.

SECTION 1
Getting Started

CHAPTER 1

What Is your Stupid?

Stupid is as stupid does.

—*Forrest Gump*

THE FIRST THING YOU NEED TO DO IN ORDER TO FIX YOUR stupid is to figure out exactly what your stupid *is*. After all, how can you fix your stupid unless you know what it is?

At times, we all make decisions from our stupid minds instead of taking time to focus on or think through something. Therefore, I am defining being stupid as living your life from one knee-jerk reaction to another. Living life that way is not being aware in the moment or focusing your thoughts; instead, it's spinning out of control in your mind. This causes chronic fictional thoughts that are influenced by past beliefs and patterns.

Being stupid is also when you think and make life decisions based on beliefs that aren't necessarily true. For instance, a client who is in his sixties shared with me that when he was a child, he was taught that sitting in the rear of the plane was safer than sitting up by the nose, so he always chooses seats in

1

the back. Once, when his boss offered him a first-class ticket for a long flight, he turned it down, not only giving up first-class service but also separating himself from the rest of the company's management team. This is an example of using a learned belief system that is not true in reality, but it was his truth. Using your stupid mind can cause you to not reach your true potential.

We are all stupid when we make decisions or take action based on past emotions or beliefs we were taught, rather than tuning in to what we may truly desire or need right now. Stupid, to me, is living life *not* in full alignment with what I want now. If you want to be healthy, but your mind ignores nutrition and just goes for burgers, fries, and pizza every night, then that is stupid. If you want to be wealthy but continue to empty your bank account and overspend each month, again, I call that stupid. I want you to live the smart life—the good life—having all the health, wealth, and love you deserve, and you do deserve it all. I want you to live the life of receiving and having all your desires by allowing them into your life.

Stupid Is as Stupid Does

I bet if you talked to anyone who has seen the movie *Forrest Gump* and asked that person to recall two of Forrest's famous sayings, he or she would say, "Life is like a box of chocolates," and "Stupid is as stupid does."

The latter phrase is genius, actually, delivered to Forrest by his mom when he was doubting and judging himself for how he communicated with others.

I sense the screenwriters got the idea from "Handsome is as handsome does," which appeared in J. R. R. Tolkien's *The Lord of the Rings*, or "Beauty is as beauty does," from Herman

Melville's *Billy Budd*, a phrase which can be traced as far back as the fourteenth century. "Handsome is as handsome does" basically means that true handsomeness or beauty has to do with a person's behavior, not his or her face.

Forrest's mom's version of the saying means that stupidity is not just a surface thing derived from a person's intelligence or how he or she speaks. Stupidity is a matter of deeds. For me, it comes down to this: judge people by what they do, not by how they appear.

The Urban Dictionary defines the phrase this way: "Stupid is as stupid does" means that "an intelligent person who does stupid things is still stupid. You are what you do."

And that is the central nervous system of the entire body of this book.

I know this to be true for me. I go stupid when I react to a situation with negative self-talk and negative conscious thoughts. It is clear to me that when I have limiting or negative thoughts, I see situations through a skewed lens and do not get the results I want. That is stupid!

Here's what happens when you go stupid. Your stupid thoughts lead you to

1. focus only on things in your current reality instead of the potential you have in your life; and
2. make decisions from your reactionary self, your negative self, and your stupid self, which keeps you where you don't want to be.

The bottom line is that what we think about is what we speak about, and what we speak about is what we bring about in our lives.

You *Are* the Center of Your Universe

Imagine I am shouting to you from a rooftop, "You are the center of your universe!" Why is that important at this juncture of the book? Because it's key that you don't ever compare your stupid or your smart to anyone else's—especially the teachers or coaches from whom you are striving to learn. Remembering that everyone I've ever known has stupid and smart parts of their lives has helped me to be not so hard or judgmental on myself.

As a doctor, I have the privilege of listening to patients share their deepest secrets with me. These patients often tell me that they have not told their secrets to anyone else. This is just one example of how we only see what people want to show us. You cannot compare yourself, your situation, or your reality with others when you don't know the whole picture. And that also goes for what you read on social media sites. What people share on social media may not even be authentic. What's authentic is what you know about your own intelligence, behaviors, and attitudes and your own mixture of stupid and smart thoughts and actions.

Everything you want to know and how to get there is already inside you.

For that reason, it's important to listen to your inner guidance system for the best way to take care of yourself and move in the direction that will take you where you want to go. As you proceed though this book, you will continue to fix your stupid, and the way you think about your entire life will change. For instance, you may be financially set but missing some very important things in other parts of your life, such as good health or the love you deserve. With the help of this book, you may discover the following:

- You sacrifice your quality of life to try to make other people's lives better.

   If that's true, you will understand that you cannot get sick enough to make a sick person well, or become poor enough to make a poor person rich, or unhappy enough to make someone else happy. The lesson, as you become smarter, is not to compromise your values to please others.

- Bettering your life will help both you and the people you care about.

   As a child, you may have heard, "The world doesn't revolve around you." Wake up! Your world *absolutely* revolves around you. You are the center of your universe.

Taking these beliefs into your life will remind you that fixing your stupid is a great opportunity to grow, without any judgment or comparison to anyone else.

Now that I've given you a glimpse into what your stupid is, I'd like you to take a self-awareness assessment to learn more about your stupid thinking and behavioral patterns.

Fix-Your-Stupid Assessment Test

The following test will help you begin chapter 2 with more information about yourself—information of which you may have not been aware. Remember there are no right or wrong or better or worse answers. Breathe deeply as you reflect on the questions. My wish is that you will learn more about how fixing your stupid is a great opportunity to help you.

I designed this test to help you determine where your stupid thinking is prominent so you can be smarter! By *smarter*, I mean thinking the best thoughts and making the best choices, to live the happiest life you can. The smart I am talking about here has nothing to do with IQ or how well you do in school. The smart I am talking about is being in alignment with who you are as a person. Being smart in this way is the only way to true happiness.

But what is happiness? Happiness is the balance and the culmination of three key areas of our lives: health, wealth, and love. By being smarter, we can increase each of the three areas and balance all three aspects of happiness. We are all smart in at least one of these categories. And I feel we can all be smarter in at least one of these areas in our lives. Figuring this out will help you start forming smarter thoughts, and what you think about is what you bring about in your life. Your current reality is a reflection of your dominant thoughts, each and every day.

Read each statement and reflect upon it. Do your best to admit whatever is true for you, with no judgment. This is just for you to reflect on patterns where you may find it beneficial to change. Most important, be honest with yourself. Score each question with a number, 1 through 10, with 1 being "never" and 10 being "always."

1. I take responsibility for everything that happens in my life—the good and the bad.
2. When I desire something, I focus more on what it's like to have it instead of the absence of it.
3. When I feel an impulse, I act on it quickly.
4. I bring whatever I desire and speak about into my life.
5. I generally look at the positive in every situation.
6. I practice a morning routine that sets the tone for my day.
7. I remember to take care of myself first so that I can inspire and give more to others.

8. I listen to my feelings to guide me in the direction I want to go.
9. I remember that when I want something, it is not the physical thing I want but the feeling of having it.
10. I take the time to feel what it would be like to already have what I want.

You can take this test at the following website and get results emailed to you: www.fixyourstupid.com/assessment.

Now take a moment and reflect on how you feel about your responses to the test. What did you learn about yourself? Once again, this is not a test with right or wrong answers. This is an opportunity for you to pause and self-reflect on any behaviors or beliefs you would like to change that would be beneficial to you. For instance, if you discovered that you are not listening to your gut feelings, maybe it's time to stop ignoring them. Or if you felt uncomfortable when you realized that you take care of everyone more than yourself, this might be a wake-up call to do more self-care.

There are no good or bad scores. This is an opportunity to objectively look back and see what is working and where there is room for improvement. Scoring 1–3 means this is an area on which to focus. You may want to read through this book and only deal with and focus on the issues with this score. Then come back and test again to see your new score. Chances are you will have a higher score and thus have a new focus. Read through the book again with new focus on the next lowest score, anything from 4–7. Lastly, go through the process one more time, focusing on any questions on which you scored 8–10.

This book is kept concise intentionally, and it's meant to be used over and over again as a way to live a smarter life. Some people may do the process I described above once, and some may keep repeating the process to get to tens across the board. All I want is for you to live your best life ever—whatever that is for you.

You Can Fix Your Stupid

Here's the good news: you can fix your stupid! The greatest thing I have found about life is that we can learn our best moves by experiencing what we want and what we don't want. Once you decide to fix your stupid, I suggest you follow these steps:

1. Think about what you want in your life right now. If you're thinking about something that you do *not* want, consciously focus on the opposite of that. This is called *pivoting*. Pivoting is being conscious about what you are feeling and intentionally changing your focus. If something happens in your current life reality that you do not like, take a minute and intentionally focus on the opposite of that feeling. Try to focus and feel what the opposite would be like if it was in your reality now. For example, say you need more money, and you feel scared or in need or poor. Take a minute and focus on abundance. Think of a time when you had more than enough of something. Keep that feeling for as long as possible. This pivoting will help you move toward where you want to be.
2. Slowly feel the change in your vibration and how you think and feel as you focus on your desire. Each day will show improvement.
3. Notice any inspiration or gut feelings that come up. The more you practice focusing and pivoting, the more in

tune you will be with inspirational ideas that will lead you in the right direction.

4. *Listen* to your inspiration and gut feelings. Do not take any action until you are inspired to do so.

5. Notice whether the thoughts and feelings around your desires are manifesting into steps you can take right now.

To take this even further, close your eyes and picture your life as it is now.

1. How do you want your life to be?
2. What would your perfect life look like?
3. Where do you desire to live? What does your house look like?
4. How much money do you have?
5. With whom are you living?
6. What vehicle are you driving?
7. What does your body look and feel like?

Now that you have answered these questions, the smart approach is to tune in to how each of your answers feels. Everyone has different goals and aspirations. There is no wrong answer here. Your goals and dreams are personal and based on your life experience. There is no goal too high or too low. It is all individual. You don't have to know the *how*; that's your job. The universe will figure out the how and lead you there through inspired thoughts that will direct your actions.

How you feel will guide you to the good life you want and deserve. How does each aspect of your perfect life feel? If you want a certain car, how does it feel to hear that car's engine start? How does it feel to sit in the driver's seat? How does it feel to drive that car? Here's a secret step that is very important: don't talk about your goals too early. If you do, people might talk you out of them. Let the momentum build before sharing your goals with anyone.

When fixing your stupid, you do not have to figure out the *how* of getting what you want. You only have to know your destination or what you want and how it would feel to get there. Your job is to decide what you want and then focus on how that feels. When you boil it down, it's really just the feeling you desire or need. Thinking about the physical desire will bring you to a better-feeling place, and that better feeling will bring you the physical things that you want. People say that seeing is believing, but in the reality of creation or manifesting, believing is seeing.

All you have to do is listen to your inner self and follow the guidance you receive. The guidance will be sent to you in the form of emotions, which are just another one of your senses. These senses, however, interpret the vibrations of the physical world. This could be called your sixth sense. Normally, you only think of using sight, smell, taste, touch, and hearing to interpret the physical world around you, but you can feel and tune in to an emotional aspect too. Just as your physical senses interpret waves of light or sound, your emotions interpret the waves of energy that supply your direction.

The key is to appreciate what you have and feel for what you want. If you focus on what you have but allow yourself to feel *un*happy, you are focusing on the lack of what you have, and you will just get more of the same. If you focus, however, on what you have or what you want, and you feel abundant, then you are on the road to more abundance.

In my chiropractic practice, I often see patients stuck in a stupid circle or cycle. Some people want to get out of it, but some people want to just stay in it. Many times, even though we have wants and desires, it's too uncomfortable to let ourselves move in that direction, but we have to make changes to get changes. Most people will keep themselves chained to their current versions of their lives. For example, when people go to a motivational seminar, they may get temporarily excited and motivated to make little changes, but they do not stay consistent enough to build momentum or make lasting change. Then old habits set in, and the next day, anger, frustration, depression, and/or despair may overwhelm them. They might get motivated to wake up early or eat better, for instance, but after a short time, the motivation wears off, and they slip back into old habits. Then the cycle starts over.

When asked what we want, most of us will spend our time talking about what we *don't* want and why. Remember that the universe listens to you and provides everything you think about. The universe does not hear the negative portion of your statements. When you say you *do not* want to be poor, the universe sees you thinking about being poor and gives you more of that. You might have heard this saying: "Don't pray for patience because you will get more situations in your life where you need to learn more patience." When you say, "I want more money," and you feel abundant, the universe takes you in that direction.

This works in 100 percent of your life, 100 percent of the time, in 100 percent of every situation.

Recently, two male patients came to my office within a few days of each other with similar problems in their backs. They were about the same age, and each had had back problems for years. Their conditions slowly were getting worse, and that stopped them from doing things they liked to do.

Essentially, I had two people who were the same physically with the same problem—with one big difference. The difference was what they wanted. One wanted to change his life, while the other seemed to only want confirmation that he had a problem and that it was never going to change. They both went through the same care plan, but guess what happened? The person who wanted to get better *did* get better, and the person who didn't want to get better *didn't*.

Manifesting in the Smart Zone

In the coming chapters, I will show you how to use your mind and emotions to manifest the life you desire and deserve.

It does take discipline to focus your thoughts. You can do it, but simply speaking, it's like a snowball effect—the better things get, the better they get. The same is true in the opposite direction: the worse things get, the worse things get. This is largely controlled by your thoughts and feelings because those two things drive your actions. This is only true because as things get bigger, you notice them more and begin to expect those things to keep happening.

The minute you start to expect things to happen, the universe answers you. When your life is running like lukewarm water, you often don't have enough motivation to make changes. When things finally get bigger, however, you begin to take notice. We mostly learn what we want by experiencing events and situations that we don't want to repeat. The bigger the things we don't want, the bigger and better things we do want.

The questions that remain are these: What are you willing to do to be happy? Are you willing to pay attention to how you feel and what you think about it? Are you willing to *not* be around people who bring you down?

Einstein defined insanity (your stupid) as "doing the same thing over and over again and expecting different results."

In this first chapter you have discovered what your stupid is. I hope you also understand that your stupid is a good thing. Your stupid mind takes you down the negative path, but remember that you only know what you want by knowing what you don't want. You likely would not appreciate great health if you never had been sick. Appreciating riches in your life is not as sweet if you never have been without things you desire. You can only feel and know true love when you have felt the opposite of that, such as loneliness or hatred.

The questions and affirmations at the end of each chapter are to stimulate you to apply what you have just learned. I want you to begin to fix your stupid right away! Remember to repeat the three affirmations 108 times.

Take time to answer the statements below. Take the smart feeling that comes up in the second statement, and keep that feeling while you say the affirmation and visualize your better, smarter life.

1. Name a time when you did something and felt really stupid because of it.

_____

_____

_____

2. Name a time when you did something and felt really smart because of it.

_____

_____

_____

3. Affirmations and Visualizations

I am committed to a better life.
I am in charge of my life.
I enjoy vividly focusing on my goals each day and feeling the results of those goals in my life.

CHAPTER 2

Our Human Blueprint: Why We Have a Built-In Stupid

For every reason it's not possible, there are hundreds of people who have faced the same circumstances and succeeded.

—Jack Canfield

NOW THAT YOU KNOW MORE ABOUT WHAT I MEAN BY YOUR "stupid" and have had the opportunity to go a little deeper into your patterns of belief, let's look at how we are made up as humans and what influences the choices we make.

This chapter is about how we modern humans still compute and react to situations, similar to how our ancestors did. Unfortunately, most of us were not taught how we operate from the inside out. Over time, we have learned, through introspection of our successes, how to manifest or create deliberately. Our ancestors were able to survive by reactions. They were able to thrive through inspired action. We all have beliefs that we were taught when we were younger, and they

15

influence our inner direction by creating expectations. I'd like to share a story about taking in ideas and concepts that perhaps may be new, foreign, or even weird to you.

At a Wendy's, Somewhere between Columbus, Ohio, and Nashville, Tennessee, 1982

I was six years old and on a long drive with my mom, which we did frequently. Mom moved us to Ohio from Tennessee so she could go to school, and like clockwork, every eight weeks, we would drive to Tennessee on Friday night and return to Ohio on Sunday. On those long rides, we had many conversations. Looking back, I now wonder how a woman in her twenties had gathered so much wisdom and why she was imparting it on me, the blond, six-year-old boy in the front seat of her Volkswagen Scirocco, while heading down the highway.

One night we were sitting in a Wendy's for dinner. My mom looked straight in my eyes with such love and said, "Son, you don't have any idea what the things I am telling you about now may mean, but one day, all of it will come together and click. It will all make sense. I promise."

That one sentence from my mom has been an anchor for me. It made me realize that we are not always going to fully understand what we hear or read right away. You can't figure out the why or the how without the full perspective of the big picture.

As a child, I did not know why or even what she was telling me. I just listened and trusted that what she was telling me was true. After all, I was a kid with wide-open ears. As children, we are naturally smart because we have not yet been influenced by the negative, stupid, and reactionary world. Unfortunately, as we grow up, we lose that childlike openness. We spend too much time as adults in trying to figure everything out—the how and the why.

One of my hopes is that you will remember and always discern your desires, as some of your desires or attachments might be born from negative situations. Let go of the "How can I make this happen?"; then the universe, your higher self, or God will provide the path for you to create and allow those desires to show up in your life. This path is given to you in the form of emotion—called inspiration. As you read or listen to the information in this chapter, it may not always make immediate sense to you. Trust, however, that as you dive deeper into yourself (via this book), the aha moments will increase, and you will gain a better understanding of how you tick as a human being. This will help you live a smarter life, feel better, and enjoy all that you desire. Be patient with yourself, and trust that the new thoughts and concepts that you hear in lectures or read in books will sink into your consciousness at the right and perfect time. Think of each book, podcast, blog, or seminar as a stepping stone and puzzle piece. Each will fit into place, allowing the picture of your life to become clearer and provide more definite direction. Your successful thoughts and practices will always be successful and lead you to new creations.

The Gift of Consciousness

As humans, we have been blessed and gifted with consciousness, which is the ability to be aware, cognitively, of what is going on within us, as well as observing outside situations. Our consciousness also enables us to distinguish what is good for us and what may not be. This shows us the best way to change a situation for the better. Our consciousness is the center of our universe.

The difference between being stupid and being smart is how much we allow our conscious minds to tune in to our higher consciousness and understand to what it is alerting us. The key words here are *tune in*. When you decide that you want to hear a certain radio channel, you use the dial to tune to that station—and this is no different. You would never get mad that you are tuned in to classical music when you want to listen to rock. You would just change the channel! It's the same with life, and when we are clear and awake to this, we make smarter, more beneficial choices.

However, when we do what I call "living blindly," we unconsciously bump from one thing to another in our careers, relationships, and overall physical and mental well-being. *Living blindly* means approaching life in a reactionary way, which means you live life as if you were playing life inside of a pinball machine. Think about it—when you put coins in a pinball machine, you enter a universe where you have to react to every move the silver ball makes. You can get frantic, wildly pushing your flippers as you try to keep the ball from approaching danger, while circling up on ramps and bumping into obstacles along the way. You will chase the ball, over which you ultimately have no control, just as you may do with your life.

In fact, similar to pinball, you may get caught up in reacting to something that happens outside of you, and in that case, you are reacting to a moving ball—one that you're trying to keep from going down the hole. That could mean bouncing from relationship to relationship or doing the flavor-of-the-month diet that you saw on TV versus listening to what we doctors of chiropractic call our "innate intelligence." Your innate intelligence is that part of you that is connected to source energy, God, or universal intelligence, and it's called many things by many people. Some call innate intelligence your soul. Your innate intelligence is connected to universal intelligence. Being smart is listening to inspiration from your smart mind. Being stupid and acting like a pinball game is the same as trying to please everyone around you at the same time and be happy too.

Of course, I am in no way suggesting that your life is not working or is bad. I'm saying that your life can improve dramatically. If you work to understand that, at times, your reactions are caused by blind spots, past experiences, and disconnecting from your consciousness, then you will see that this can be costly and detrimental to creating your most precious desires in life.

All of us, at times, are run by our stupid; we react to physical stimuli and make decisions without thinking. Remember that living the good life is happiness. True happiness is a balance of three things: health, wealth, and love. At any given time, we are always smarter in one and stupider in another. We all have the spirit/God/innate intelligence within us that sees the bigger picture and can guide us to what we want, but the stupid part of us makes us focus more time and energy on the problem and blaming others instead of accessing that innate intelligence and focusing on our greatness. What you think about, you bring about. If you focus on your stupid, you will do stupid things. Most people, unfortunately, only wish half-heartedly for the things they want, and they settle in their careers, health, or relationships because they listen to their stupid thoughts, which are sometimes called beliefs, logic, or even reality.

There are three areas in which people want to be smarter.

- Some people are unhappy with their bodies and may want to make a change, but they listen to their stupid minds and decide they can't make the needed changes or they don't know how.

- Other people may want to have a million dollars or a Ferrari. With half-hearted wishing, they will quickly be discouraged, as they cannot see how they ever could afford such a car.

- Still others want that perfect relationship but think more about how they always attract the wrong people.

This is where people get lost and why they lose hope and give up—they think they need to know the how. But the how is not theirs—or yours—to figure out.

If you focus on the feeling of your desire, you will be inspired, step by step, to get the *how* done. In fact, once you know that you have a stupid and a smart, it becomes a very specific choice to stay stupid and unhappy. Most people spend more time finding excuses for why they cannot do something than actually doing it. This is called *arguing for your limitations.* Our current reality is whatever we can hear, taste, touch, and smell, right this second, and it's based on our past choices. Our future reality, however, is based on our vision ahead. It's how we choose to feel. It's what we choose to focus on. It's how we intend to react to each segment of our day. If we react based only on our current "today" reality, then we will never change our future reality. We are either in alignment with our desires or out of alignment. When we're out of alignment with our desires, then we are out of alignment with ourselves, and we feel bad.

This is where you might spend lots of time and energy trying to figure out how something will happen. Getting too caught up in the details will knock you out of alignment every time. It is important to stay general with your thoughts about your desires until you have built up enough momentum to get more specific without losing your alignment.

Most people feel they have to make choices for their current reality. Let me give you an example: a single mother who doesn't receive child support might have to get two minimum-wage service jobs to pay her rent, but what if her dream is to be a registered nurse? To fulfill that dream, she'd have to work the two jobs while she went to school. The trick is for her to focus on the feeling of being a nurse. It is not for her to figure out the exact *how* in this moment, as that will kick her out of alignment. She will argue for her limitations and stay right where she is. This is living in the stupid mind. This may seem overly simplified, but it's easier than you realize to reach your dreams. In this example, if she only focused on becoming a nurse and why she wanted that, she could be inspired to take actions that would lead her down that path to that goal.

Getting more general in your thinking will help you feel inspired thoughts that point you in the right direction. To get more general, ask yourself why—why does this mother want to become a nurse? We always want what we want because we think we will feel better when we have that. Look for the bigger feeling. Does she want to help people? Does she feel it will bring more money and allow an easier life with more freedom? There is always a way to your goal, no matter what happens each day. It's like the GPS in your car. No matter how far off track you get, the GPS will gently remind you at every turn to head in the right direction. You can always get back on track. I think about the times I thought I'd never complete college or attract the relationship of my dreams. I was thinking stupid because, in reality, I achieved both. It's amazing how we can argue for our own limitations instead of our unlimited possibilities.

The lesson here is that our stupid runs our lives when we think our innate intelligence is something separate from us instead of something that exists within. I know firsthand about that, especially in terms of balancing my relationships and professional career. Like that pinball, I used to bounce around off the bumpers of life, thinking I needed to be everywhere at once. I would get obsessed with building my chiropractic practice to provide a better life, sometimes to the extent that my family suffered. Only years later did I realize I was stuck in a no-win situation. My nervous system, or smart self, was sounding loud alarms at every request I received, but instead of listening, I reacted, and I believed I needed to be everywhere at once. I felt that forced action would get me what I desired. I felt I could make it happen if I worked hard enough, if I pushed hard enough.

Sometimes that caused me to miss out on everything and fail to show up at all.

There are two kinds of action: *forced action* and *inspired action*. Forced action is like the pinball game. It's often the kind of action you have been taught to believe in. You may have heard, "No pain, no gain." That is forced action; it's hard, and it ultimately will cause burnout. With the forced-action plan, people feel they have to work hard and sacrifice to get what they want. They often feel guilty for enjoying life. Eventually, the push of forced action will catch up with them. For example, if they're trying to get heathier by working out and they push themselves harder and harder, they eventually will burn out or even hurt themselves and have to stop working out altogether. As a physician, I treat people daily who overdid something with their bodies—on the ski slopes or at the gym—ignoring their limitations.

You might have a good run or a high score once in a while, but it's not sustainable. To have a successful life, you must realize that it is not just about hard work. Working harder is not the answer in itself. This is where "work smarter, not harder" comes in. You must connect to the power, the inspiration, to act in the right way, and *then* work hard. Inspired action never feels like hard work; it feels like fun. You can vacuum all day long, but if you're not plugged in to the electrical outlet, you won't get any results, regardless of how hard you work. After all, your goal is to feel better and be more satisfied and happier, not just do busy work.

In my early practice life, if someone at my office needed something or if a patient called, I would drop everything at home and run to the office. I had a belief that I needed to work hard and sacrifice to be successful for my family. I was under the false belief that says, "No pain, no gain, and you can't have it all." My mind was like a yoyo that had me on a string of stupid thinking. I was constantly reacting to circumstances in life—and feeling out of control. My answer to everything was to work harder. I felt I had to earn my piece of the pie before someone took mine. This was stupid. The smart me knew there is unlimited abundance in the universe, but so many motivational books and gurus focused on working hard and sacrificing. This led me to focus on the bad things happening in my world, which in turn led me to expect that those bad things would be realized if I did not sacrifice and work hard—and in many cases, they were realized anyway.

Remember what I said before—what you think about, you bring about, no matter if it is what you want or what you do not want. Whatever you focus on is what will grow. By focusing on working harder, I was creating a life of harder and harder work. This was initially satisfying because I felt young and thought

I would put my nose to the grindstone and "make it happen." I didn't realize that all I needed to do was *allow* it to happen.

Anything can happen if you let it.

—*Mary Poppins*

What Was Missing?

I didn't realize that my stupid was running my life. I was too busy trying to figure out the how of it all. Instead of staying present with my wife and children and communicating what was going on at the office, I ran into the fire, working harder and harder. Even though I had a good excuse, I felt disconnected as a family. I can only imagine that my family must have thought they were second in my life. You probably won't be surprised to learn that my stupid actions eventually led to divorce.

My stupid was reactive instead of proactive; I didn't listen to my smart. Instead pausing to assess the situation and look at my true priorities, I ran as fast as I could to work on problems that didn't necessarily need an immediate fix. I was reacting like a pinball. I worked very hard to be successful but at what cost? I could feel that I was leaving my family behind and that we were becoming more disconnected on certain levels. I worked even harder to fix it. *Stupid!* Hindsight is always 20/20, and working hard, especially with blinders on, is not the best action. I want to be clear: everything wasn't going bad because I was working hard, but working hard was not leading me to the good life. There was no balance for happiness. True happiness is a balance of health, wealth, and love. Reacting was the only mode of operation that I'd known through my entire life. Most people do not naturally check their emotional guidance systems first. Most people push their feelings aside or hide them deep down.

Wise sailors used the North Star, or Polaris, the brightest star in the night sky, to navigate their ships to safe ports and plot their courses. I had no North Star, no clear direction on how to navigate situations. My stupid had no idea which direction to go to get me anywhere. I had no compass or map—until I discovered my own inner navigator, my innate intelligence.

Being aligned with my innate intelligence is exciting to me. It gives me direction, like the North Star, and allows me to work smarter, not harder. The more I focus on being aligned and allowing the inspiration to flow, the more my life improves. This allows me to access a higher consciousness and to be inspired.

Focusing on your feelings should be the hardest work you do. An easy trick for this is to use short meditations to quiet your stupid mind and allow for smart thoughts to flow. You will gain several key benefits. When you react less and listen to your inner knowing more, taking inspired action, benefits will include the following:

- You'll understand and break loose from non productive mental and emotional patterns.
- You'll have an increased awareness of your emotional reactions, many of which are rooted in childhood experiences that created your beliefs.
- You'll gain more understanding of how past traumas and wounds drive your thinking and actions today.
- You'll stay focused and zero in on your desires and action steps to manifest them in three key life areas of happiness: health, wealth, and love. This is the good life we all want to live.

- You'll take responsibility for your reactions and results instead of blaming others or outside circumstances.

What you think about is what you speak about, and what you speak about is what you bring about."

—Dr. Fred Schofield

Dr. Fred Schofield, founder of Schofield Chiropractic Training seminars, is a chiropractic consultant who teaches energy management. His seminars and teachings are what began to wake me up. Everything he taught resonated with me; it felt right. Growing up, I always felt the presence of a higher power or higher self. I have named this part of me, which is still me but also separate from me, my *smarter self*. This is where I began my deliberate search for the good life.

What Dr. Schofield's powerful quote, above, means to me is that you have to be 100 percent proactive, not reactive, and listen to your inner calling and go for what you dream of, desire, and deserve. Life is about creating, attracting, and getting what you desire. The purpose you came to this earth is to expand. This means that you are here on this earth to grow; to experience a better and better life; to feel better and better. You do this through living contrast.

Contrast is having opposite feelings and situations in life. By living life, you learn about what you want and what you don't want. Being poor or not having enough money will lead you to desire the contrasting opposite—having wealth or more money. Being sick will teach you the desire for health. Contrast, or feeling a lack of something, is where all your desires come from. You don't have a preordained path; you came here to expand and grow. Each time you feel contrast, you clarify your desires of what you want in life. This gives you direction.

I remember a time in my life when I finally took full responsibility for all situations in my life. Good or bad, I would look at every situation and say to myself, "I did that."

When you remember to stay laser-beam focused on how you want to feel, that will inspire you to take actions that will give you better results. This ultimately will change your behavior, which will change your life. The real work—and only "work"—you need to accomplish is to stay focused on how you want to feel, which will lead you to being inspired to the best action. Once you receive inspiration from your higher self or source energy, you are plugged in to the power, and now you can do so much more with less effort in less time. Without plugging in, it is like you are vacuuming your floor without connecting the vacuum to the electric socket.

Nature as My Teacher

One day, as I read how some mother birds get their babies to fly out of their nests, a light went on. All I ever knew was how to react to situations and force things to happen, but the mama bird had a much better way. When the mom felt her chicks were ready to fly, rather than pushing them out of the nest, she flew to a nearby tree and called them. She never stopped calling, and eventually, they flew to her. I see the mama bird as our smart selves, our inner knowing, our souls, our God consciousness. It's a guiding force that will never stop calling us in the direction of our desires.

I thought, *Instead of pushing against what I don't want and forcing action on what I want, ranging from more money to better health, I should listen to which direction my inner spirit, my guidance system, wants me to go.*

Our inner guidance always knows the shortest path to get us to the things we want. Like the mother bird, my inner guide didn't need to push me toward my desires. Our inner guides always are calling us to the easiest path that we are ready for. After I had that realization, I began to quiet my mind through meditation, taking deep, slow breaths that originated from my belly and gently exhaling them through my mouth, like a big sigh. This stopped the noise and helped me listen within for inspiration and guidance. In that centered state, I realized that I didn't have to react and fly before I was clear about where I wanted to go. Like the birds, I listened for the calling and then flew.

It's not your job to figure out how to get where you want to go. Just listen to your innate guidance system, which is calling you, and, like the mama bird, it will guide you where you need to go.

Our Human Guidance System

The next step to understanding how to fix your stupid is to take a look at how you operate. It is much easier than you think.

You don't need to know the ins and outs of how your car's engine works, just as you don't need to do any work to make the engine go. All you need to know is how to turn it on, press the gas, and then use the steering wheel to take you places. A car's navigation system lets you know where your car is now and how to get to the next place, and the same is true of the navigation system within you.

Think about this—when you get in your car, has your GPS ever talked to you about your past? Does it ask you where you have been or get upset if you make a wrong turn? Of course it doesn't. Your car's navigation system only cares where you are right now and where you want to go next. It just follows your thoughts and instructions. And if you start going the wrong way, it will put you back on course or react to your changing the coordinates of the destination.

Your human guidance system is innately within you in a very similar way. The key to success is directly related to how often you remember to access, interpret, and harness your inner guidance system.

Let's look at our inner GPS, which has two key systems.

Your Emotional Guidance System (EGS)

As you know, humans have five senses: sight, smell, taste, touch, and hearing. Each of these five senses interpret some type of vibration. These five senses help us get through each day and interact, enjoy, and navigate life. They help us determine what we like and what we don't. These are our preferences for life.

Think of your emotions as your sixth sense. Your emotions also interpret vibration and show you what you like and don't like as well. They show you your preferences for life. And they will tell you if you are heading in the direction of alignment with or away from what you want. The first five senses allow you to interpret and understand your current reality; emotion is your guide to your future reality.

One of the biggest secrets for living the good life is to harness all six senses in combination with each other. This will help your happiness—your balance of health, wealth, and love. Most people use the traditional five senses but ignore or downplay the sixth, which actually is the most important sense. When I access and focus on that sixth sense, my emotional guidance system (EGS) helps me feel confident, happy, and calm and leads me to make smart decisions instead of stupid ones. I share this with you because we all have this compass to help us bridge our emotions and our physical minds and bodies. It also shapes and expands our view of physical reality. You might refer to your EGS as your inner voice, higher self, or gut feeling.

Your EGS Is Your Starting Point for Creating What You Want

Esther Hicks is an inspirational speaker and author. She has coauthored eight books with her husband, Jerry Hicks. Together, they have presented Law of Attraction workshops for Abraham-Hicks Publications in up to sixty cities each year since 1987. Through meditation, Esther has been able to tap into a source of higher consciousness that she has named Abraham. To me, this source of consciousness in the nonphysical dimension is the starting point for how we attract or manifest what we desire in the world.

When you are in tune with your EGS, you are consciously aware of your emotions. This is important because your emotions guide you. Just like your car's navigation system, they signal when you are heading in the wrong direction, away from your goals.

Reticular Guidance System (RGS)

Your reticular guidance system (RGS) plays an important part in how you walk through your day, as it controls how you perceive the world. Your RGS serves as a filter to bring about what you think about. Let's say you decide to buy a new car—and suddenly, the car you desire seems to be everywhere. For instance, when you leave the grocery store, the car you've been thinking of is parked next to yours. As you bring the image of the car into your mind even more, day after day, something starts to happen. You don't realize that the car was always there, but now your filter is set to bring it to your attention and allow it in.

Could it be that things you want in your life were always around, but you filtered them out of your consciousness? Quite possibly. When you focus your energy on a specific object or goal, you are emotionally guided toward it. The mental constructs you have had for years, however, may still try to take you in a different direction. As a result, when you activate your RGS to take you toward your goals, old filters will have less power over you.

It's important to use both of these components of your human guidance system together to get to where you want to be as quickly and easily as possible. The best way to use these guidance system components is to quiet your mind and allow them to take over. For instance, imagine trying to listen to your car's GPS while your teenage kids are arguing in the back seat. One competes with or drowns out the other. To help you practice quieting your mind and getting centered, take a moment to enjoy one of my favorite simple and very effective meditations, which I use daily.

Focusing Your Brain Meditation

1. Commit to take fifteen to twenty minutes, and turn off all computers, phones, and other distracting machines. As an optional step, I like to turn on a fan or another kind of white noise, and focus on that. YouTube has lots of free meditation sounds.

2. Take three or more slow, deep breaths in and out of your nose.

3. Focus on whatever emotions you are feeling right now. Take a moment to pay attention to any feelings you may be having, from sadness to anger to joy.

4. As you continue to breathe in an out, release any negative emotions that may arise.

5. Take a few more deep breaths, and notice whether you feel more focused now.

6. Spend the rest of time releasing all thought. Keep your mind as empty as possible.

I suggest that you make an appointment with yourself to do this meditation each day. Take at least fifteen minutes, and relax, quiet your brain, and center your thoughts. This allows you to feel inspired as well. Remember that consistency builds momentum. If you miss a day, don't give up, just start again tomorrow.

You cannot talk and listen at the same time. All day long, you talk to the universe about your preferences and what you want. If you never take the time to listen, you cannot be guided to what you want.

Even if I have to pull into a parking lot to do this meditation, I will do it. The shift that occurs within me and the enhancement to my ability to listen to my EGS is well worth fifteen minutes of my day.

Consistency with meditation also builds momentum. The more days in a row you take the time to meditate, the faster your results will come—in fun and magical ways. You will be surprised and delighted. Many things that happen each day pass you by because you are so busy asking and talking instead of appreciating and listening. When you force yourself to get quiet, you are more likely to experience the inspiration to take action at the right time.

For instance, when I get on the congested freeway after meditating, all of a sudden, the best passing lane opens right up. Then, my office manager calls me to tell me several of the overdue patient checks we were waiting for came in, and we didn't even have to call to remind them. Instead of my usual pattern of driving one hundred miles a day, back and forth, between my two offices, I realize after I meditate, through inspiration, that I don't have to react to every little glitch and run to fix it. By focusing on how I want things to be, I am able to relax and be inspired to take the best action.

It takes space, time, and repetition to focus and refocus your thoughts and feelings on how you want your life to be. It helps to understand that today is your past, and how you choose to feel about a situation helps you create your future reality. And by the way, when I don't rush in, my staff often is able to fix a problem themselves. And the kicker is that when I rush in with stress, I sabotage myself because they feel my vibration, and the job doesn't get done as well. Remember my pinball machine analogy? My staff and I both do much better when I meditate, as compared to when I start hitting the flippers and bouncing off bumpers. It's like hammering a square peg, over and over, trying to force it into a round hole—until it breaks. Forced actions just don't work as well as calm, focused ones. The stupid things you keep thinking about are the stupid things you keep talking about are the stupid things you keep bringing about.

You don't have to reverse your thoughts or change your beliefs; you just have to think about something else so you can be open to creating a better result. And that's what quiet meditation does. If you made a wrong turn on your trip, you would never feel the need to drive back to the starting point.

You would just pay attention to your car's navigation system from where you were and keep heading toward where you wanted to go.

Sometimes the Best Action Is Distraction

If you are all knotted up over something in your life, you will only be able to focus on the negative, the stupid, or the lack of what you want. The best way to shift or make a change to being smart is to distract yourself. Go do something that will allow you to reset. Take a nap, go to the beach, work out, or do whatever it takes to allow you to be in touch with your smart self. Remember that only what you pay attention to grows. This means that when you spend time thinking about what you do *not* want to have, be, or feel, you are allowing that to grow. Albert Einstein once said that the energy of the problem is different from the energy of the answer. Once you stop thinking about the problem and only feel what it would be like to already have the solution, you can revisit your previous issue with new clarity and guidance.

It's all about vibrational energy. With the help of my RGS, I can feel my energy highs and lows. The negative filter through which I was seeing life was blocking me from noticing solutions that were right in front of me. As I raised my vibration, I stopped hearing messages that were confusing. It was like having two totally different genres of music playing at once, so in reality, I couldn't hear either. When I distract myself with things that make me feel good, my body relaxes, my fingers and toes tingle, and I feel as if I am the center of my universe.

I also find that when I am in sync with my own vibration, I draw people into my life that have similar energy, purpose, goals, and inspirations. Likewise, if I am feeling a discordant type of energy, or I'm angry or afraid, I call in people who feel the same as I do. It's as if I have a virtual basket of energy within me, and when I fill it up with stupid thoughts, I change my vibration to match those. The good news is that it means I can also turn it around and think smart thoughts, which sets off a positive vibration that will make things flow toward me instead of away.

Positive emotions also give you feedback that you're in the process of manifesting something you desire. Negative emotions could be trying to sabotage you or give you a warning signal to listen deeper. In *Ask and It Is Given* by Jerry and Esther Hicks (2004), Abraham Hicks teaches that your emotions are your soul's way of telling you whether what you are focusing on aligns with your higher self's desires.

The lesson is that you have the power, through quieting your mind and feeling for inspiration, to create the environment that will help you attract what you desire.

Now that you have experienced my fifteen-minute quiet meditation, go to www.fixyourstupid.com/meditations to download the audio version with relaxing music, which you can use as your daily practice.

1. What is one time in your life when you clearly listened to your inner guidance system and had a positive experience?

   _____

   _____

   _____

2. What is one time in your life when you tried to force action but got only a negative result?

_____

_____

_____

3. What do you do to distract yourself and feel better?

_____

_____

_____

4. Affirmations and Visualizations

I am at peace, happy, and satisfied.
I believe in myself.
Inspired action is the active ingredient that transforms my goals into my reality.

CHAPTER 3

How to Switch from the Stupid Zone to the Smart Zone at Will

Everyone thinks of changing the world, but no one thinks of changing himself.

—Leo Tolstoy

A Hot Summer Day in Orlando, Florida, 2017

As I shared earlier in the book, I am obsessed with learning the best ways to grow and manifest as a human. I have attended thousands of retreats, workshops, and courses on many aspects of human development, led by many amazing teachers.

One day, I was at a seminar on the law of attraction with Abraham Hicks (the name used to define the alignment Esther Hicks has with Abraham, whom I mentioned earlier). Esther and her husband, Jerry, who died in 2011, taught together worldwide. Now, Esther continues this work alone but with inspiration from Jerry from "the other side." The Abraham-Hicks Workshops are held all over the United States in almost forty cities every year. Participants can ask Abraham-Hicks any questions they want. The answers are then channeled through Esther Hicks and communicated with clarity and wisdom.

One evening, I was listening to people ask similar questions over and over.

"Where is my stuff?"

"How do I get more money?"

"Why can't I ever have a successful relationship?"

"Why am I suffering from this sickness and can't get over my health issues?"

This was nothing new, and I usually would still learn from every person's situation, but something bothered me this time. That *something* was making me think we were sitting with one of the most tapped-into and infinitely intelligent sources I had ever experienced. No matter what question the audience asked Abraham, they got the same answer. Abraham said that we all want something—no matter what that is—because we think we will feel better by having it. If we could stop focusing on where the answer is and instead focus on the feeling we truly desire, then the situation will come about. It is impossible for it *not* to do so!

Inside, I felt something begin to stir. I thought, *Would you all stop asking the same questions? This is why your health or your romantic or financial lives are not changing.* People asked questions but didn't listen to the answers Abraham gave through Esther and Jerry Hicks.

I sat quietly and was inspired into a new and higher thinking. When I left the building that day, I was amazed at the changes in my thinking. I made a shift. I expanded. I thought, *Why can't*

we all remember to listen to our inner, less-judgmental selves? After
all, every answer Abraham gives is the same at some level.

The message is that no matter which areas of your life you
want to improve, you have to change your vibrational energy
first. Rushing to or forcing your solution, rather than focusing
on why you created the problem, is your need for immediate
gratification. Your stupid wants that immediate gratification,
which often leads to long-term negativity in your life, while
your smart wants long-term positivity.

Sometimes the immediate, forced, quick fix does not lead
to long-term health, wealth, or love. We need to understand
why we create problems in the first place. Albert Einstein once
said that if he had one hour to save the world, he would spend
fifty-five minutes (of alignment) defining the problem and only
five minutes of action, finding the solution.

Einstein illustrated an important point: before taking the
action of jumping into solving a problem, we first should invest
time in improving our understanding of the problem and our
desire for the outcome. Using only effort to try to solve problems
will only make them bigger. There is the energy of the problem,
and the energy of the solution. You cannot keep focused on the
problem and get the solution.

As I remembered Einstein's view toward solving problems, I
realized that most people, including me, can be stupid at times.
We ask the same questions over and over and get the same
answers, but we avoid really hearing them. The majority of the
people in attendance that day most likely had been listening
to Abraham speak through Esther and Jerry for years and had
read all their books, but they still kept asking the same old
questions. There needs to be a shift from asking and putting
energy out to letting the answers in.

The Puzzle Pieces Finally Fit Together

That day, something clicked for me. I laughed at the realization that came to me—if I could be that stupid, why couldn't I be that smart? I felt a sense of purpose run through me. I said to myself, "I need to let people know how to stop doing what they're doing and make a real change."

For me, it begins with the realization that to fix my stupid, I have to stop the momentum and the direction in which my stupid mind is taking me. Changing the direction of your thoughts might take some time, but eventually, you will steer yourself in a smarter direction.

Have you ever watched airplanes landing on the runway? It takes about a mile for them to turn the aircraft around and go in another direction. The pilot must be patient and allow the plane to slow the momentum of going in one direction before he can change to another direction. Like the airplane, we may need to let our thoughts run their course for a mile. In order to move in a smarter direction—toward our destination—we need to catch those stupid thoughts, slow them down, and turn them around by focusing on the opposite thought—the positive thought.

Once you realize that you first need to go the extra mile to turn your thinking around, you then can accept situations as they are and take full ownership as the pilot of your life. This will also help you have patience while fixing your stupid. Fixing your stupid is about living the good life—having lots of balanced health, wealth, and love—and the best way to do that is by taking charge and directing your thinking.

Here are some steps to help you stay on track with your thoughts and desires:

1. Set the direction in which you want to go. Realize that you are the nucleus of all the thoughts you have, which gives you the control to steer them to where you want.
2. Draw a line down the middle of a piece of paper. On the left side of the paper, list all the stupid thoughts you have that you don't like. On the right, fill in your opposite, smart thoughts, or what you think they should be.
3. To fully turn your mind around, fold the paper in half, and read only the smart thoughts on the right side. Then fly in that direction.

This is the *pivoting* I mentioned earlier. The side on which you choose to focus will determine where you wind up.

To end this chapter, I want to offer two reminders: First, be easy on yourself, as your life is a journey that brought you to right here, right now. There is no right or wrong. Life offers an infinite number of branches for us to grab on to. Second, look at your folded sheet of paper whenever you feel discouraged or overwhelmed; it will help to keep you on your smart path.

1. What is one positive area in your life for which you take responsibility?

_____

_____

_____

2. What is one negative area in your life for which you take responsibility?

_____

_____

_____

3. What is one thing you are willing to do to make a change and be smarter about it?

_____

_____

_____

4. Affirmations and Visualizations

All that matters is what is happening right now.
I am creative; I act creatively; and I feel creative.
I act on inspiration from a quieted mind.

SECTION 2

Taking Action

CHAPTER 4

Manifesting in the Smart Zone

Instead of worrying about what you cannot control, shift your energy to what you can create.

—Roy T. Bennett

YOUR "STUPID" MIND AND PEOPLE WHO LACK CONSCIOUSNESS both will tell you that wanting is bad, but that is not a good mantra for you to hear when you are trying to manifest your soul's desires. When you want more—as you were designed to do in life, starting from birth—your stupid will tell you that you should *never* want more. It will persuade you to be satisfied with what you already have with thoughts like, *You are better off than so many other people in this world, so stop desiring more.* Take a moment and think about where humanity would be if we were all satisfied with where we were and never tried to progress. For starters, I guarantee you would not be reading this book. Our reality is based on learning what we desire through contrast. Contrast creates new desires, ideas, and growth. If our society did not embrace the contrast and keep moving forward, life, as we know it, would cease to exist.

Living a Life of Contrast

I have lived a life of contrast almost my entire life. I grew up in a religious environment and was taught that any desire was greedy and selfish. Obviously, not all religions have this belief, but I heard repeatedly that I should be content with what I had and ask for nothing more. It felt like a sin for me to desire anything. I kept telling myself I should be content with my current situation in my relationships, my business, and my health, no matter what. I was taught to be happy, content, and complacent, which, for me, boiled down to being *stupid*.

This cannot lead to the good life. You cannot truly be free with this thinking. When you open your mind and free your thoughts, creation abounds.

It is our true nature to be inspired to want more. Our true nature is to create. For instance, when I listened to people around me and accepted the bad things that happened in my life, I kept feeling bad, but when I was inspired, and followed that, I was led to something better.

My parents got divorced and moved 1000 miles apart when I was and infant. When I was fifteen years old I would walk three miles to work. At one point I held three jobs. During the week, I worked at Walmart, and on weekends, I opened up Taco Bell and closed Arby's. I hated walking that distance to jobs I didn't like, and I always felt unstable about where I was living. One week, I stayed at my grandparents' and another at my aunt and uncle's. As bad as my life felt, however, I always knew what sort of life I aspired to live, and it was quite different from the life I was living.

Those years of feeling unsupported and tossed around motivated me to get more out of life instead of continuing with the spinning hamster wheel I found myself on daily. Had I not had those experiences, I never would have developed a strong desire to live the best life ever. Negative experiences, like I had, often motivate us to create new and better directions in our lives. Negative experiences can create greater focus and determination. And as I've mentioned, your built-in guidance system will guide you there in the easiest way possible.

Manifesting Does Not Need to Be a Struggle

Abraham Hicks has monthly recordings from seminars and often teaches that living life as I was runs counter to our souls' desires. Once I heard this message and started following it, my life changed for the better. Yours can too! And the greatest thing is that each person on the planet can focus on whatever thoughts he or she uniquely desires and always have them realized. Where would I be today if I hadn't wanted more? I firmly believe we all came to this earth to create as much as possible *and* to enjoy that process of creating.

With that in mind, let's look forward to where you want to see your life going, and leave the past behind you. After all, you can't drive a car forward while you're looking in your rearview mirror. Focusing on the things in the past means you're focusing on your stupid. The past is what got you to where you are now, but it will not get you to where you want to go next. Focusing on your past sets you up to repeat the same patterns.

Your current reality is your past. That's because all your past feelings, decisions, and choices have created what you have today, right now. What you choose to think and feel and do right now—this second—is creating your future.

Here's what I suggest: Appreciate all your experiences, and realize that each moment of your life helped you to get where you are. Changing your stupid to smart *now* will give you the new and improved future you desire.

And here's the best part: when you manifest your new and improved life, you will think of new inspirations and desires that you want next. Life and creation are like trampolines; you can use your current situation to give you a bounce in the right direction.

Here's another secret: if you stop and listen to your soul's desires, there will be no end of your creating more and more of your desires until the day you die. I mean that the better it gets, *the better it gets*. Each new creation that comes to fruition in your life will inspire further creation.

Look at the evolution to technology, for example. Every year, computers and phones get more powerful in what they can do. Each invention and goal reached leads to an inspiration to go further. It can be the same for you.

You Are Designed to Give More Too

Look around—many hospitals, universities, and mental health facilities are built by donations from wealthy people who have the means to serve their communities and the desire to give back. We are a creative society that believes in innovation and progress, so we want to keep improving, whether that means more efficient cars or faster computers or better medical devices. We are part of a universe that is always expanding. And as part of the whole, we too can expand with our thinking. The more we expand our ability to stay open to our higher consciousness, the more creative, loving, and healthy our lives will be.

Think about some of the great inventions that benefit you daily. Our mobile phones are more powerful than the first supercomputers. We used to carry paper maps in our cars to find our way. Now GPS voices tell us each and every right or wrong turn. If we were meant to be satisfied with cooking on a fire over rocks, we would have stayed there. Seeing us as expansive humans in a universe that is also expanding may help you understand why we are advancing mental and physical technologies, exponentially faster and faster. As higher-consciousness individuals, we also instinctively know that the faster we expand, the faster we spark the desire for further expansion.

You have the power to turn any object of your desire into reality. This is why you have a guidance system that guides you through your emotions. If you desire to get a new house or car, think of how you will feel in that new house or car. In your mind's eye, go through the process of actually purchasing it—not the how of it but the feeling of it. It's a challenge because after a short time, you might fall back into your stupid thinking; it's common to get busy and forget to return to that higher, optimistic feeling. We can forget that we are creating our future when something in our life shows up and knocks us down,

In order to change that, you need to realize that what knocked you down is just something from your past playing out. You then should get back up and keep moving forward. Always forgive and keep moving in the direction of your desire.

We could make two mistakes at this point. First, we can get lazy, lose focus, and then expect our desires to show up without focusing through meditating or listening to our original desires. Another common mistake is that we stupidly take for granted the things we have already created. This stops us from being able to expand into a healthier, wealthier, and more loving state. Let's be very clear that creating and manifesting should not take hard work or be difficult. The hard work is done by the higher perspective. Our work is to focus on what we want and why we want it, without thinking about the lack of it.

It may not seem easy when you start, but as momentum builds, it gets easier. And you always have your two-part guidance system to redirect you and guide you to those desires. It does not matter where you start or what detours you take. It doesn't matter if it is money, relationships, or an object, like a house or car. You must remember to find your way back to that feeling of already having it in your life as much you can.

As you move into what you want to manifest in key areas of your life, remember to enjoy the process of fixing your stupid. Also enjoy that fact that in every minute of every day, you can make a choice to feel, act, and do something smart—or something stupid. That's a very key part of this process.

Contrast in your life will create desire, and a feeling or an inspiration will spark inside of you. As the feeling of what you want gains momentum, you will think about it more. As an inspiration from the bigger, nonphysical part of you, it can go in only one of two directions. This is based on whether you will have smart thoughts, which will lead to a positive feeling, action, and result, or stupid thoughts, which will lead to a negative feeling, action, and result. It is really that simple.

You are on this earth to improve, my friend. There is no limit to how smart you can be.

In Which Areas of Your Life Are You Smarter?

Let's discover where your stupid and smart show up most in different parts of your life. Where you are now in your health, wealth, and love was influenced by learned beliefs. Your beliefs came from your life experiences. For instance, you may be living on the smart side financially because of the way you were raised. Wealth or abundance may have come naturally to you if you were taught to or expect to be smart financially. On the other hand, you may have grown up in a very supportive home where you experienced unconditional love continuously, which means you're now attracting and keeping love. That may come easier to you than those who never saw love modeled to them.

Each stupid or smart decision you make in life is a step up or down the manifestation staircase. There also are landings on that staircase, where you can stop to enjoy your smart decisions and what they have gotten you or to regroup to stop your downward descent. Either way, commit to the process and keep reaching, as it always stimulates growth and your creative abilities.

In the next three chapters, you will have the opportunity to assess and change any stupid actions from beliefs that are getting in your way. This will allow you to have all the key areas of your life humming at full power.

You must think and focus only on the positive. It's not as simple as just quitting stupid things. When you focus on stopping something, you are still focused on the negative. Focusing on the negative will get you more of that exact negative. The bottom line is that you get what you think about, whether you want it or not. More often than not, we spend more of our time thinking about the things we *don't* want than the things we *do* want.

I'd like to explain a sneaky little thing that can trip you up with this. When things in your life don't go as well as you would like, it often can be frustrating. You may think you are being positive and only thinking and talking about the things you want. You may affirm that you want more health, wealth, or love, using optimistic words. It may look very good from the outside, but you may be coming from a place of lack. When you talk about having more money, you might be focusing on it from past experience and a place of lack instead of *feeling* abundance and appreciating the many things you have that are abundant. Your feelings might be centered around the lack of abundance instead of the confidence you can create and allowing more to flow into your life.

To gain momentum in moving toward the things you want, you must feel the results you desire, and then hone in on that feeling. Your guidance system will show you the way. Always remember that you get do-overs. You start fresh every morning, with the chance to reconnect, restart, build momentum, and try again.

I coached a chiropractic client who was stuck in his stupid mode. He had been practicing for years but was stuck in a rut. The more we talked, the more I realized why he could not get what he wanted. He kept focusing on—and expecting—the same negative results he had been manifesting. He was stuck in his stupid and living in a world of excuses.

George Washington Carver said, "Ninety-nine percent of the failures come from people who have the habit of making excuses." My client did not realize he was expecting to fail. He just made excuse after excuse for why he could not succeed. He was expecting problems, so that was what he kept producing.

Initially, he argued for his limitations, convinced that his problems were because of outside influences he could not control. Once I helped him to see that results are based on what we attract, he was able to make some changes. He had to change his focus and his habitual thought patterns. He couldn't just get rid of his stupid thoughts and habits; he had to replace them with more productive habits. I suggested that instead of waking up and feeling nervous and fearful about his day in the office with his staff, he should start his day by feeling what it would be like to have the office he dreamed of.

Remember the folded-piece-of-paper idea I discussed earlier? My client followed that concept—he wrote everything that he feared about his practice on one side and then wrote the opposite on the other side. He wrote what his dream office would be, using perfect detail. Then he started each day by visualizing and feeling emotions of success, happiness, and fulfillment.

By starting his day with smarter thoughts, he was able to feel better. Once he did that, things began to turn around. He changed his focus and, therefore, his feelings. He plugged his destination into his emotional guidance system and realized that good things already were happening in his practice. He could see the daily wins his office produced—once he focused on them. His practice started to multiply and grow, and it wasn't long before the success he wanted came to fruition.

And guess what? It wasn't just his practice that succeeded; his relationship with his family improved too.

1. What is one way you thought you were acting positively but actually felt lack or negativity?

———————————————————————————————

———————————————————————————————

———————————————————————————————

2. There are three aspects about the good life of living in true happiness—health, wealth, and love. Which aspect has been the hardest for you to achieve, and which has been the easiest? Why?

_____

_____

_____

3. Which aspect of your life do you want to change the most? Why do you want to change it? What is the true feeling or desire behind it?

_____

_____

_____

4. Affirmations and Visualizations

I live my life on a want-to-choose to basis by being happy and satisfied. This creates the power and enthusiasm in my life every day.
I am powerful, positive, and constructive.
I see myself achieving my goals.

CHAPTER 5

Creating the Health you Dream Of

Success is the sum of small efforts repeated day in and day out.

—Robert Collier

As a chiropractic physician for over twenty years, I can say that health is interpreted in many ways. Almost everyone has a formed belief of what health looks like and feels like. For instance, I've seen patients who believe that as long as they can get up off the sofa and walk to the refrigerator, they are healthy enough. On the other hand, there are CrossFit enthusiasts who push every aspect of their bodies to the limit.

Your perception of what "good" health is depends on several factors, including your emotional state, your belief systems, what your parents may have believed about health, and much more. As you will see in the examples that follow, you should not compare your standard of what good health means with anyone else's. That's thinking stupid!

You Are the Center of Your Own Universe

I want to explain how important *you* are. The world *does* revolve around you! You, as a person, are extremely important. In fact, you are the most important person in your life—and there's a reason why. When you are on an airplane, and the flight attendant goes through the safety procedures, he or she will tell you to put on your own oxygen mask before you help anyone else. It's a wise policy because if you don't take care of yourself and get some oxygen flowing so you can breathe, you can't possibly help anyone else. I had to learn that lesson as a doctor myself.

A few years back, I had some patterns that were affecting my body and health. When I became tired, I was in the habit of grabbing anything to eat to pump up my energy as quickly as possible. My belief was that as long as I had energy for my patients, I was doing well in my role as a doctor. Meanwhile, I ignored how my body looked and felt. As long as I was able to down some food and keep going at full speed all day, I believed I was healthy enough. I felt that I would always be able to do better in the future—once I achieved some of my other goals.

That thinking, however, didn't work. I started working longer hours, missing workouts, and didn't even walk or stretch. I continuously fueled my tank with fast food from places like Taco Bell and Wendy's. I was stuck in a cycle of drinking coffee all day until I was headed home for dinner. After the kids were in bed, I finally had a chance to sit down to eat dinner and relax. At that point, I could easily down a bottle of wine to offset all the coffee I'd drunk, just to help me get to sleep. I was in full stupid mode.

At the same time, I was trying to train my mind with affirmations and positive thinking, but what I was really doing was being positive for everyone else, while inside, I felt negative. I was focused on the lack of the time and freedom I really desired. I might have seemed super-positive and inspirational to my patients, but inside, I was beginning to resent parts of my life.

Eventually, it all caught up to me. I had kept myself from acknowledging that my pants size was going up, and my belly was hanging over my belt. I woke up tired and sometimes hungover. When I saw myself in the mirror, I noticed my face was puffy. As a result, I often avoided looking at myself in the mirror.

I also was going through life by reacting to everyone else. I thought of myself as a people-pleaser, a helper, a doctor. Remember, though, if you don't put on your oxygen mask first and take care of yourself, you can only last a limited time, trying to take care of others.

I wasn't tapping into my smart, so not only did my physical health suffer but my mental health as well. I was sluggish, and because I wasn't moving my energy, the anger I felt inside backed up and came out at people I cared about, like my office staff. After a few weeks, my staff got fed up with it and started pushing back. It hit me square in the face. I thought, *I have to change, or I'll lose everything that I desired and worked so hard to achieve.*

As I sat at home one weekend, contemplating how I could get myself out of my stupid mental and physical trap, I realized that I had to quiet my mind and begin to listen within. I knew I had a guidance system, and I needed to use it—pronto. I needed to practice what I was preaching to my patients and clients. I was spending every second of the day talking and asking and pushing. I knew that in order to make a change, I needed to do the opposite of everything I was doing. I needed to be open to my feelings and be guided by inspiration.

As I sat still, taking slow, deep breaths, I started to visualize my higher consciousness, my god self—the "smart" Carl. I saw a bright orange sunrise, with me under it, walking along a path. I was doing my daily ritual of walking for thirty minutes before I jumped on the phone or went into one of my offices. In my mind, I saw myself sitting down and calmly eating a healthy breakfast of fresh fruit and a couple of eggs. I was enjoying a delicious, nutritious protein smoothie instead of gulping down coffee. I saw myself getting dressed and looking at how nice my pants looked on my lean waist and fit body. I was seeing the smart me. And I even remembered times when I had felt like that before.

This is where I developed my folded-paper idea I discussed earlier.

I opened my eyes and took a few notes; then I went into my old photo-album collection. I found a photo of me prior to my living out my stupid ways. I saw a physically fit, happy man, excited to make his big mark on the world. That night, I committed to stopping this stupid lifestyle and felt as if I had broken free of beliefs that were keeping me unhappy in almost every area of my life.

Each day, I saw the lean, mean Carl photo, which I had hung on my closet door. I spent most of my free time focusing on what my higher self would do. I asked questions in that quiet state. I would wait to take any action or make any decision until I felt I had received inspiration on which actions to take and when to do them.

Inspiration comes first in the form of emotion. Positive emotion equals the right direction, and negative emotion is the wrong direction. I learned to not take any action unless I had a strong emotion to do so. If there was any question, then I waited. In this receptive mode, I received answers to my questions. Those answers guided me to make a plan of action.

I immediately felt better. I decided that I would let that feeling be enough. Within weeks, I saw tangible results. I felt better about myself, and people told me I was more accessible and that they felt better being around me.

Over the next few months, I lost thirty pounds. I changed my diet from quickly eating anything handy to eating well-thought-out meals. I loved having healthy, yummy smoothies or oatmeal for breakfast and salads and soups for lunch instead of greasy fast-food pizza, tacos, or french fries. I felt comfortable in my clothing; nothing hugged my body, and I didn't have to be embarrassed about my belly showing. To be totally honest, I lost that uncomfortable feeling of hugging people and feeling my protruding belly pushing against them. Overall, I felt more comfortable and confident than I had in years.

You Deserve to Create the Health You Desire

1. Take a moment to relax, breathe, and allow yourself to quiet your mind; then ask your higher self to show you a vision of your healthy, smart self.
2. Ask your higher self to show you inspired actions to improve your health.
3. Take a moment to imagine how it would feel to have your health desires realized.

In my chiropractic practice, I employ the above three steps with my patients. Your beliefs about your health are key to how you can heal. Your beliefs about your health begin at a very early age. After all, a belief is only a series of circumstances that you have seen or thought, over and over. If your parents had an illness or complained often about how they felt, then you may have adopted a similar relationship to your own health. A big part of my role in my practice is to help patients change beliefs that are negatively affecting their ability to feel better.

Steve Sisgold, author of the book *Whole Body Intelligence* (2015), coined the term *viral beliefs*. Sisgold says,

> Like infective, corrupting agents that sicken our bodies, viral beliefs sicken the mind and negatively impact behavior. Just like those pesky, parasitic, protein-coated virus molecules, viral beliefs can lie dormant until some external factor or emotional trigger activates them. ... Most viral beliefs are falsehoods, distortions whose power lives in the past. Viral beliefs are not true in the present moment, but they sure do feel real. Because you believe a viral belief is real in that moment, your body responds with the same biochemical signal it did in the past, saying that you are in danger and that you need to protect yourself as best you can. As long as viral beliefs go unexamined and live on in the body, they can trick you into acting in counterproductive ways.

For instance, viral beliefs tricked my patient Sarah, who believed her "bad" back stopped her from playing golf, which was something she had cherished doing for many years. Golf also allowed her to spend time with her husband and friends. It was a very big part of her social life now that she was retired.

I would ask her, "How are you today, Sarah?"

Her response was always the same: "Doc, I can't play golf anymore because of this darn back. I used to play eighteen holes but can't even get through nine now. I am really frustrated because I keep gaining weight, and I have stopped doing my aerobic classes too."

Of course, Sarah had pain, and I empathized with her, but I also saw that her stupid was at work. After all, I had looked at her x-rays and test results. Her physical body did not match her feelings. I concluded that Sarah had fallen into a trap of focusing on her negative beliefs and not seeing that she could do something about her health condition instead of just complaining and giving up. The first step was to discover where this belief system started for her.

In Sarah's situation, I helped her realize that she was latching on to her stupid thinking by focusing primarily on her suffering instead of using her smart self to discover what she could do to make herself feel better. Of course, I could help her with chiropractic adjustments, and I did, but I was still concerned about her giving up and settling for poor health and her inability to walk the golf course or go to an aerobics class. I knew what I had learned about my own stupid self, and because I'd taken the time to fix my stupid first, I wasn't about to let her stupid mind convince her that her enjoyment of her physical life was over.

Typically, in my practice, most patients simply have a mechanical problem in their spines. With a few adjustments, they are back to their normal lives. Due to Sarah's seemingly emotional ties, however, I decided to dig a little deeper with her. We explored her beliefs about her health. Remember that beliefs are just thoughts that are repeated until they become part of the internal belief system; they are not necessarily true. Sarah said that her mom had taught her that health naturally diminished when you aged. There was nothing you could do about it; it was just part of life. Sarah also had a firm belief that she was destined to a life of suffering and that, ultimately, there was no remedy that would ever get her back to enjoying golf or other activities.

The advantage I had was that she was already a patient seeking pain relief and was open to digging a little deeper. She really wanted to get back on the golf course and into the gym. I helped her see that she was choosing to focus on the problem only. I also shared that the more she perpetuated those thoughts, the longer it would take her body to heal and be out of pain. Sarah learned that her thinking was as important as the treatments she was receiving. She agreed to partner with me on fixing her stupid by accessing her smart more.

We began with my guiding her on how to do simple meditations to take control of her thoughts so they wouldn't control her life. I taught her to take deep breaths and close her eyes, while seeing herself on the golf course, hitting golf balls. I asked her to imagine the warmth she felt when the sun shone on her face and even had her sense the smell of fresh-cut grass on the greens. She smiled and said she felt happiness when she did that.

I continued by asking her to feel each feeling and share it with me. She said that she felt energy moving in her body; she felt more relaxed and a general feeling of happiness all over. I then explained that we all have a guidance system that guides us to where we want to go. I also reminded her that her higher self had brought us together so she could heal and enjoy moving her body again for years to come. I wanted her to realize that she was in control always.

Sarah began to see the difference between how her stupid mind and her smart mind made her feel. During every visit,

I gave her an adjustment and included visualization exercises. After a few weeks, she began to do visualization at home and saw improvement.

I explained that she was orchestrating her healing, and because she had been persistent with her desire for a better life, she had been shown the path to getting better. I then explained that consistency would build momentum toward her goals; that it was not about perfection in execution of the plan or path but consistency with being in better alignment with her greatest desires.

She had less pain and began to take walks at night. Within one month, she went to the golf course and started putting the ball around. After three months of fixing her stupid, she was able to play a round of nine holes of golf. She was ecstatic, and so was I.

Like many of us, Sarah was blinded by her current reality. She got caught up in her pain and suffering and the beliefs that her mom had taught her; she never took the time to step back and take control. She needed to realize that her current reality was based on her past experiences, while her future depended on what she chose to do in the moment. Once she made that choice, she was back in the game of life—and golf.

Sarah's story is just one example of how your feelings and emotions are your guidance system, which makes you the creator of your reality. By reacting to your current suffering or challenge with your stupid mind, you also unleash emotions that create more suffering. You must be willing to see your current reality as something that's not permanent but as a trampoline to jump on, launch yourself, and motivate you to create what your higher self knows and desires to be true.

Action Is Inspired Energy, Not Work

Now let's get you started fixing your stupid by exploring any beliefs you may have around your health. Take a moment and pause. Breathe slowly, and focus on any beliefs you have about your health right now. What did you come up with? Is that belief boosting or hindering your health?

For instance, are you feeling bad that you are diabetic and not following your recommended diet? Or are you ashamed about the size of your waist? What feelings come up about your being stupid when it comes to your health? If you could rewrite any beliefs about your health, which ones would you choose?

For instance, if you want to change the belief that your heart is not strong, affirm that you have a healthy, strong, beating heart. Let go of any health beliefs you may have inherited from family, such as that your family has weak digestive systems. And last but not least, close your eyes and see a photograph of you shining bright, in your most perfect health. Take that feeling into today and every day. It will help you change your stupid to smart and improve your health as a result. You will receive inspiration on what to do.

1. Where in your life did you learn your beliefs about health? Do they serve and align with your current desires?

_____

_____

_____

2. What is the single most important aspect of your health you would like to change?

_____

_____

_____

3. What is one step or choice you can make each day to consistently move toward improving your health or achieving better health?

_____

_____

_____

4. Affirmations and Visualizations

I have an unlimited supply of positive energy that allows me to enjoy the health I desire.
I recover easily and effortlessly.
I am active and receptive to life.

CHAPTER 6

Having the Wealth you Deserve

It's simple arithmetic: Your income can grow
only to the extent that you do.

—T. Harv Eker

To fix your stupid to manifest the financial wealth
you desire and deserve, let's begin by focusing on abundance,
which includes money and a whole lot more. From the air you
breathe to the sun on your face to the relationships you enjoy,
you live in an abundant universe! Looking at the world you live
in through an abundant lens will help you focus less on what's
missing and gain more satisfaction within.

You cannot look forward and backward at the same time.
If you are driving your car, just imagine how many accidents
you would get in if you only looked in the rearview mirror. You
would not have any idea what you ran into; what stopped you
from moving forward. This is the same with your abundance.

When we get stupid and forget how abundant the universe is, we dam things up and block the wealth energy from flowing in. Abundance is not about dollars at all. Abundance is truly about freedom; we just tend to focus on dollars. Our lives are spent wanting things and trying to figure out how to get the dollars to buy what we want. From toys to houses to cars, we work hard to create those dollars. We often do not let abundance flow into our lives. Instead, we hold on to limiting beliefs that have been in our heads since childhood. Instead of allowing abundance to come to us by feeling abundant, we focus on the *how*. It's the universe's job to give us the *how* through inspiration.

We have other things in abundance to focus on. If those things don't come to us easily, it's because we don't know how to create wealth. On the other hand, when we have no resistance or negative beliefs about something, it will show up easily. In truth, creating a castle is as easy as creating a button. Try finding something simple to create, as I did, described below.

One day I was listening to Esther Hicks on YouTube. She was discussing blue glass, butterflies, and feathers in relationship to abundance. I started to focus on those three things instead of an abundance of dollars so that I could get into a receiving and attracting mode. I discovered that once I let go of dollars and focused on creating and seeing abundance all around me, a shift happened.

I suggest that you take your mind off money and choose something else to create in abundance for now. Once you get in the creating-abundance mode, amazing things will start to happen. Remember that everything around us is eternal, and by changing your vibration, you will receive more abundance and happiness in your life. The wealth will come, but you have to be available to receive it. Too often, people spend too much time complaining about the money they don't have instead of being open to receiving more.

The amount of abundance in the universe, including on our little earth, is unlimited. This means there will never be a shortage of whatever anyone truly wants. Think about how old this earth is and that there are not any new shipments of supplies coming in daily. Everything we have here is unlimited and ready for us once we are ready.

T. Harv Eker, in his book *Secrets of the Millionaire Mind* (2005), says,

> I'm a big believer in the universal law that states, "What you focus on expands." When you are complaining, you are focusing on what's wrong with your financial life, and since what you focus on expands, you'll keep getting more of what's wrong. Many teachers in the personal development field talk about the Law of Attraction. It states that "Like attracts like," meaning that when you are complaining, you are actually attracting "crap" into your life.

People with a positive mind-set around wealth, on the other hand, can become wealthy in any economy.

One of my mentors, Steve Sisgold, told me about one of his clients, who owned five bookstores. When Amazon and high rents put most bookstore chains and practically every independent store out of business, his client decided to open even more bookstores. He equipped them with cozy children's sections, an abundance of art books, and top-shelf organic cafés. People who love to stroll aisles, touch and look through books, and buy one and enjoy a cup of coffee with it responded well. His business is booming; he believed in his idea and attracted wealth, despite what the rest of the world was doing.

You Are Connected to the Universal Supply; Think of Your Life as a Hologram

A hologram is a three-dimensional projection of an image. If you break that hologram in half, however, you will still see the entire image projected, just smaller. Even if you can break it into quarters or eighths, it will still display the same whole image.

My point is this: the power you possess as a human, even when parts of your life may not feel abundant, is your ability to connect with the vibration of the entire universe, where every part of the whole is also within each individual. Like the hologram, even when you feel like you are broken, you still are connected to the unlimited whole, which has enough wealth and abundance for everyone.

Connect with the universal vibrational energy, and you will ride that wave to financial and other types of abundance.

Creating abundance means learning to stay longer and longer in the smart zone.

Animals Know How to Live in the Smart Zone

Look at how animals attune themselves to the vibrational frequencies around them. For instance, watch how a dog feels and smells its way through life. It just listens, feels, and follows energy and vibrations, rather than pondering anything.

You too can live more of a sensory life, where you feel and connect with the vibrations that will take you to where you want to go. You have lots of practice living life with your five well-accepted senses that allow you to accept reality. Smell, hear, taste, touch, and see—this is what you are used to doing. But feeling emotion means interpreting a vibration that is unseen. It takes practice and getting used to it. We have lost touch with that and have forgotten the importance of interpreting emotional vibration.

Of course, living this way may be a brand-new experience for you. In time, through trial and error, when things happen, you will change the way you respond.

In the past, I allowed my stupid to control my finances. As a result, I struggled financially, didn't feel a sense of purpose, and just wasn't excited about my life. Most of my time was spent focusing on how to keep up with paying my bills instead of connecting with my innate ability to attract wealth and abundance into my life. When I thought about wealth, I didn't follow my smart mind; instead, I acted out of desperation and worry. My actions were forced, due to the stress I felt around paying bills, and it created even more debt.

Remember that for every situation, there are two ends to the stick. Think of a magnet. The polarity of one end is positive and the other is negative. The same goes with abundance. One end is positive and focuses on allowing abundance and feeling good about finances. The other end is negative and focuses on abundance going away from you.

Do What Makes You Feel Happy

One day, I noticed something. Whenever I had a day filled with patient appointments, I felt light, happy, and abundant. A profitable day did wonders for me, but I would feel down about myself when appointments slowed down.

I wondered how my wealth and business might change if I held on to the busy-day elated feeling even on slow days. That shift in my thinking from stupid to smart led me to act on inspired action instead of forced actions.

When I started my day by allowing time to meditate and listen to my guide within—my emotional guidance system and my reticular guidance system—I received inspiration for how to best attract business to my clinics. The more I did that, the happier I felt because I was connected to my higher self as my business adviser.

In order to stay in the smart zone as much as you can and create the wealth you want, remind yourself consistently to quiet your mind and let your higher self take the driver's seat. You must be persistent in this to keep reaching forward.

When you connect to your higher self, you will match the vibration of what you want to bring into your life. It gets the ball rolling—and it's a lot more fun.

Inspired Action Worked for Me

I was guided to take actions that allowed me to reverse my financial situation. Keep in mind that my situation was *my* situation, and I handled it the best way I could at the time. There are many different ways to change your situation in all aspects of the good life. Do what's right for you. For me, the first thing I did was file bankruptcy so I could clear debt and start over. I took some time to inventory my actions, and that revealed that I was forcing everything in my life. I'd lost my original spark and purpose.

My inner guide gave me a plan that my busy, stupid thinking could not hear. I listened and opened up an office in Florida; then I committed to live a life of inspired actions only. I made a commitment *not* to run to work first thing in the morning but to meditate and journal instead.

The Big Switch

My awakening came from flipping the switch from focusing on what was missing to envisioning how I wanted my financial life to go—remember that what you think about expands. As a result, I was open to seeing all the miraculous opportunities I had in my life. Things shifted almost immediately. From worry and fear, my thinking changed to optimism and appreciation.

I was in Florida, after all, and once my eyes opened, I realized that the snowbirds up north would move down my way in a few weeks, which meant opportunity. My depressive thoughts started to turn to elation. Once I was out of the stupid zone, I remembered that my sole purpose of coming to this earth was to be happy, walk the path of least resistance, and create. I also tuned in to how much I love being a chiropractor and helping people get healthier.

Once I adopted smart thinking, I went out into my community with that vibration, and referrals came in quickly. Within a few months, my income increased; I kept to my spiritual and physical practices; and I was happy again. The key here is that I got happy and satisfied first, and let that be enough. It didn't matter what happened after that. By releasing the outcome, it had to come. When I asked my higher self for something, I let go of the *how* it would happen and let go of the outcome. My only job was to focus on the feeling of it happening.

You too can keep the feeling of what you want as if it already has happened; then you will have what you want, from its naturally flowing to you.

Here's what I learned that may help you, wherever you are in your life.

1. Accept and understand that you are where you are financially because of past thoughts, beliefs, and actions.
2. List any stupid thoughts you have around wealth and change them to match the future wealth you desire.
3. Appreciate any good things that happen in your work or business. If it's just one new client or a new sales lead, cherish that and be thankful instead of focusing on what is missing.
4. Listen to your inner guidance, and remember that you are the creator of your circumstances.
5. Your EGS knows how to get you to where you want to go. Listen to it. Quiet the noise, and watch how your finances increase.

The More You Live in Abundant Thinking, the More You Can Do for Others

You must take care of yourself before you can take care of anyone else. You cannot give if you haven't received. If you really want abundance, then learn to receive. If you are not willing to receive, then you are being selfish to yourself and others. For instance, the more wealth you have, the more you can help others live more abundant lives. You can teach others, through your example, how to live in the vibration of wealth. You already have all the answers inside of you. Just focus and listen to your inner being to learn what it will take to attract and enjoy the wealth and abundance you desire and deserve—and watch it flow to you.

1. Name one thing you like about your job or business.

   _____

   _____

   _____

2. What is one thing you do to earn money that creates a positive vibration?

   _____

   _____

   _____

3. How much do you focus on taking care of yourself and making *you* your priority?

   _____

   _____

   _____

4. Affirmations and Visualizations

I feel happy healthy and wealthy.
All the money, abundance, freedom I seek is seeking me.
I constantly think thoughts of infinite supply and unlimited abundance.

CHAPTER 7

Attracting and Enjoying the Love you Desire

I believe in true love, and I believe in happy
endings. And I believe.

—Christie Brinkley

As I've mentioned, my ultimate reason for writing this
book was—and still is—to express my purpose, which is to
help my patients heal and to lift up the lives of the clients and
audiences to whom I speak and to people who read this book.
I didn't know, however, how my own life would unfold as I
wrote this book.

I really got the message that this was not a coincidence
when I realized that as I was listening to my higher self
and focusing on the creation of this book, my vibration was
changing—and so was the quality of my life. As they say, life
is a journey. Initially, I had decided to write this book to share
past experiences I had struggled with and the processes I had
learned from those, including better ways to think. As I shared

my newfound beliefs, insights, and daily practices, however, something amazing happened. As I consistently increased my focus and paid attention to my emotions, trying to look at everything through the eyes of my higher consciousness, I experienced more clarity. I got even clearer on what I wanted in my life and, more important, the path to get there. That clarity and alignment with my higher self attracted what I desired emotionally. I became more and more in alignment with how I wanted to feel and act toward myself, my life, and others. Remember that wherever you put your attention creates energy, which, in turn, draws a similar energy to you.

Every one of us can be extremely smart in some areas and act totally stupid in others. Those who may be wise and succeed in business may not be as smart when it comes to love, and vice versa. I had to change the beliefs deep inside of me that were sabotaging my ability to find and stay in love for the rest of my life. To do that, I knew I had to rewire my entire approach to love.

To further illustrate this, I will share my process for going from stupid to smart and then tell you what miraculously happened to me.

Rewiring My Stupid Beliefs around Love

The first thing I had to do, which was a hurdle for me, was to truly look at and accept my current situation. After accepting my current situation, I then had to take responsibility for where I was and why I was there. I was divorced with five children because of what I had created and attracted into my life. My position in life was no one else's fault or doing.

That is the first step—taking full and total responsibility for your situation. You are where you are, and you have been through what you have been through because you attracted this into your life. This means that your current life reality—the things in life that you can see, taste, touch, and smell—is directly related to your past feelings, thoughts, beliefs, and actions. This may be difficult to understand, or it might even seem a little harsh, but the people who have done this step have been able to move on to very healthy, productive, and wonderful relationships.

Keep in mind that fixing your stupid is not like a college degree, where once you've completed your degree, you have it forever. No. In life, there will always be ups and downs and incompletions—*ups*, as you strive for more, and *downs*, as you may regret situations. You, however, will come to appreciate the lows as much as the highs.

Discovering things you don't want will give you clear direction of what you do want and will inspire and motivate you to go and get it.

I wrote down on a piece of paper, "I accept that I have not yet created the relationship I longed for"; at that time, I was divorced with five children.

Next, I wrote down (in present tense) where I wanted to be: "I am crazy in love with a beautiful woman who is into being active, appreciates spiritual growth, and lives a chiropractic lifestyle." That affirmation alone felt very powerful and relaxed me from feeling any pressure to find that person in the near future—just the opposite. I knew I had lessons to learn, so I had no expectations as to when she would show up, but I did sense it would happen someday. I even added, "No matter how long it takes."

My higher self heard my desire, and my path to lasting love was created. Not too long after that, I got a call from a friend who asked me to housesit his place in Florida while he was traveling for a few weeks. I flew down days later and arrived in the early evening. After a good shower, I decided to grab something to eat at a nearby restaurant. It was about eight o'clock, and the place was packed. I was offered the only seat left, which was at the bar, so I took it. I sat down and struck up a conversation with a couple of women who had stopped in for a drink after seeing a show. The conversation was easy, light, and fun. I felt comfortable talking with them and especially with the woman sitting next to me. We had a lot in common, and something just clicked for me. As I look back, it clicked for both of us.

By the end of that evening, I knew without a doubt that I felt something for her and definitely wanted to see her again. By the end of that week, after spending more time with her, I realized that she was going to be part of my life.

She later told me that she felt the same that evening, and her friend had told her, "This is your type of guy."

We spent the next few days together, getting to know each other, and I was sure we were meant to be together. I realized that it hadn't been an accident that my friend had invited me to stay in Florida. Instead, it was my connecting to my higher self and listening to my deepest desires. Every other weekend after that, for several years, I went to Florida, knowing that one day we would get married. Things were easy, natural, and fun. There was no pressure or struggle. Neither of us was in a rush, but I knew that when I asked the question, she would say yes.

I also wanted to buy her the best engagement ring I could find. I looked for many months but couldn't find the type I wanted to get. I waited patiently. I was learning to trust my emotional guidance system and reticular guidance as well.

Here's the exciting news: Joann, a friend of mine, who was a jeweler, called me when I least expected it. We had been meeting off and on for several months. She was trying to help me find the right quality of ring within my budget. Her birthday was coming up, and I had already decided I would get her a nice bracelet or something and hold off on the engagement ring.

Then Joann said she had a photo that seemed to match my vision of what I wanted. It was perfect, and offered at the best price of anything else I had seen. She told me that it would sell by the end of the day, so if I wanted it, I had to get to the bank and wire money to New York. That same day, I chose a setting for the stone. A jeweler from New York set the stone and sent the ring to me the day before her birthday! I proposed that evening, and the woman of my dreams wore the perfect engagement ring I had been looking for. I was learning how to love with my smart mind, and it was heavenly.

Here's a step-by-step rundown of how I recreated my relationship to love:

1. I accepted my situation when it came to love and learned from it.
2. I made a new commitment to how I would love and act in the smart zone.
3. I realized that no one is responsible for my happiness.
4. I focused on attracting a long-term partner who was aligned with my beliefs and interests.
5. I focused primarily on what made me feel good about the other person.

The Stupid Relationship Killer

Both partners need to take responsibility for their own happiness. This takes pressure off the relationship and makes space for more love and happiness.

One of the traps we often fall into is wanting to have the feelings we had when we first fell in love and to have those feelings remain forever. When we meet someone new, we feel giddy much of the time, and that person can't do anything wrong. That's only because of where we focus our thinking. When our energy or vibration is high, we tend to ignore things that might ordinarily bother us so that we can stay in love.

I realized that if I focused on what I loved about that person, then my vibration would stay high, and she would feel that from me. We agreed that we would never blame each other for any negative situation. Instead, we would take responsibility for co-creating it and for allowing what was happening in our lives.

When we lower our vibrations or allow our energy to dip, we can get negative. We do this by looking for and picking on habits or behaviors we're not crazy about. Our vibration gets lower, and our partners feel that.

Focusing on your partner's essence and best qualities is being smart. Bringing your limiting beliefs and negative behaviors of nitpicking into relationships is stupid.

Remember that the more you take responsibility for keeping yourself happy, the more you will feel better about yourself and, in turn, your loved one. Your built-in EGS will take you where you need to go when it comes to love, and your RGS will filter what you want to see. After all, of the more than one hundred restaurants I could have gone to that night in Florida, my EGS led me to the one she was in. It is so accurate that it set it up so there was only one seat open—the one next to who I was looking for.

How Smart Are You When It Comes to Love?

As I've mentioned, using your EGS, or energy guidance system, to find the relationship you are wanting is like using the GPS in your car to reach a destination. To direct your EGS to take you where you want to go, however, means you must write down clear and specific goals. Your GPS will take you to any city, but it won't know the exact address unless you put in that information.

I took the time to detail with whom I wanted to be in love, which directed my EGS to take me over a thousand miles to a bar stool in Florida to find her.

Here are two smart steps for you to take right now:

1. Grab a pen and paper and write down three very specific traits you love and desire in a partner. For example, "I love his/her ability to stay patient with others, no matter what." Physical: "I love the softness of his/her skin." Emotional: "I love how he/she stays relaxed, breathes, and centers when stress arises." Vibrationally together: "I love how we can sit for hours and be content and comfortable with each other."
2. Write down the best attributes of your loved one.

If you have a partner, you can do this exercise together and then share your lists with each other. Make it a special exercise to advance your commitment of love to each other. It can be as formal or informal as you want, depending on your relationship. Some people take time for dinner on a weekly or monthly basis and make a deliberate effort to focus on and discuss their relationship and where it is going. This will keep programming your guidance systems to take you both where you want to go. Unless you give clear direction and plug in the coordinates together, your relationship slowly will head in different directions.

The secret to making this process successful is to start with general goals and what you see yourselves doing in the future.

Then, get as specific as you can without becoming negative. If anything feels off as you discuss your future and life goals and the road to get there, back off and find a more general agreement. Maybe you both want more freedom to travel together, and it feels good to talk about it, but maybe the details of how and when to travel bring up negative feelings or lower vibrations. If so, back off and agree that someday you will travel with fun and ease and without the limitations of time and money. If you let the more general feeling be enough for the two of you, your two guidance systems will lay out the path and filter in what you need so your dreams can become a reality. Let the feeling be enough for now.

Take turns reading to each what you wrote after each section. Notice how you perceive your loved one now? Share any awareness and feelings you have with each other after the exercise. I recommend that you do this regularly with each other.

Practice Having All-Smart Relationships

As a doctor, I know that it's important for me to be in the smart zone with all my relationships, from my vendors to my staff to new patients.

A young man named Joe was referred to me by one of his coworkers. When Joe arrived my front desk person cordially greeted him. He filled out his paperwork and was led to a treatment room to wait for me. The universe had lessons for Joe and me that day, as my staff member went to lunch and forgot to alert me that Joe was in a treatment room. After sitting for about twenty minutes, Joe came out, angry, and loudly said, "This always happens to me at doctors' offices. I have to sit and wait forever for them. I'm leaving."

Of course, when I heard Joe, I got up from my desk and went to see what was happening and how I could help. After

Joe told me what had happened, I apologized for the mishap and explained it was far from normal.

"It's important for me to help and heal and not have anyone feel neglected at my offices," I told him.

What I said hit a trigger point for Joe, who again said, "I'm always forgotten at doctors' offices. In fact, I actually expect that to happen when I walk in."

His past experiences and negative beliefs about medical appointments kept bringing him the same results.

At that moment I had a choice. I could mirror Joe, take what he was saying personally, and defend or react, but then, like him, I also would have a bad result. I realized that our worlds had collided for a reason. I could help Joe change his belief system, and he would most likely get better treatment from doctors' offices.

I was given the opportunity to raise my vibration for Joe. I took a few deep breaths and decided to show him, over the next few visits, that I was interested not only in his experience that day but in improving his life.

I also discovered that he had felt rejected and invisible most of his life—at home, school, and work. I used my own examples to explain that expecting negative things to happen brought me familiar results that I did not like, much as he had been doing. I helped him see that if he changed his negative expectation and took full responsibility for how he wanted his appointments to go, he could possibly have a better experience.

During one of his visits, we talked about his emotional guidance system and the law of attraction. Joe was willing to take full responsibility for his actions and for every situation in his life, the good and the bad. Joe liked what I was saying; he agreed that he wanted to let go of his negative perceptions and attract better results in all his relationships. I had him write down how he wanted to be seen and treated by others. Then I gave him a piece of paper and instructed him to draw a line down the center. On the left side, he listed things like, "Medical offices don't care about me and make me wait a long time." On the right, he wrote, "I am an important client to my doctor, and my time is valuable. I will be served in a timely and efficient manner."

Then he wrote down other places where he felt unimportant or rejected, such as at work, home, or with friends.

"The key," I told him, "is to fold the paper in half and just look at the right-hand column several times a day. Any time you feel a negative emotion, take out the paper and write it on the left side. Then pivot and write the opposite on the right side."

After a few more coaching sessions and, of course, chiropractic treatments, Joe shared that something was shifting. He noticed that the more he focused on having positive interactions with others, the more he felt accepted and received. And his back pain was gone too.

I learned that Joe was also a teacher for me. He motivated me to be smarter when it came to how I perceived and affected all my relationships inside my practice and my personal life. I realized that in every interaction, I can affect the outcome by the vibration that I bring to it.

1. What are your current relationship goals? What is the one thing you could do better to keep your energy or vibrations higher?

_____

_____

_____

2. In your current or past relationships, where have you blamed others for how you felt and not taken responsibility for making your relationship better?

_____

_____

_____

3. Where does your "smart" shine in your relationships? What is the best way you keep your energy or vibration high?

_____

_____

_____

4. Affirmations and Visualizations

All the love I desire is desiring me.

I free myself and my partner so I can build my relationships by knowing that no one is responsible for my happiness but me.

I am an incredible person and attract incredible people into my life.

SECTION 3

Allowing and Keeping Abundance

CHAPTER 8

Living with Intention: Taking Massive Action with Little Effort

If you really want to do something, you'll find a way. If you don't, you'll find an excuse. If you are not willing to risk the usual, you will have to settle for the ordinary.

—Jim Rohn

AT ONE OF DR. FRED SCHOFIELD'S SEMINARS, HE TOLD US about an old Cherokee legend. A Native American grandfather is talking with his grandson around the campfire one evening. He says to the boy, "I am about to share a very important lesson with you. There are two wolves inside of every one of us that are always at war with each other. One of them is a good wolf, which represents things like kindness, bravery, and love. The other is a bad wolf, which represents greed, hatred, and fear." Then the grandfather closes his eyes and is silent.

The grandson stares intently at his grandfather. He says nothing for several minutes. Then the boy clears his throat and innocently asks, "Grandfather, which of the wolves wins?"

The grandfather opens his eyes as he quietly replies, "The winner is the one you feed, child; the one you feed."

This fable is perfect at this point in the book. By now you've learned that your mind is also like two hungry wolves, and it's up to you to decide which one you will feed—the stupid one or the smart one. You also know that *you* are in control of which part of your mind to feed and that you can choose to use the skill sets you've learned in this book to fix your stupid. You've learned a bunch about your stupid mind within you, and you've also learned about the smart mind you possess. The purpose of this chapter is to build the framework for having a happy life by using your smart mind to set intentions to "feed" the three main components—health, wealth, and love—that will provide the blueprint for your happiness and success.

This is the good life that I want for you. Now it's time for you to put into action what you've learned in the previous chapters and move your life forward.

Exercise: Blueprint for a Happy Life

www.fixyourstupid.com/blueprint

1. Take a pause. Stop your thinking, and stop trying to consciously figure out everything. Take a deep breath, in and out. Affirm within that you have the freedom to create your life the way you desire it to be.
2. Notice how affirming that freedom feels. Take another deep breath, in and out.

3. Close your eyes and focus on new things you desire to bring into your life.
   * health intentions
   * wealth intentions
   * love intentions
4. Notice how each intention feels. Most likely, it feels good. See if you can keep that feeling alive in you as you proceed through the chapter.

You should do the above exercise periodically. How often you do it depends on you. Some may want to do it weekly to speed up the changes in life, but that frequency may be stressful for others, who may prefer to do it monthly. Remember you are looking to "fix your stupid."

You want a certain thing because you think you will feel better when you have it. Do not let the processes in this book be stressful or hard. Go gently with the ideas. If you have a question, don't act; instead, wait for inspiration. Trust me; it will come. You will get a feeling in your gut or a thought. It might be as simple as making a call, going for a walk, or even driving somewhere. Remember that your inspiration will lead you to the answers you are seeking by the easiest way for you to understand.

My wish is that you realize and remember that the manifestation of what you desire will magnify the good feelings you have by visualizing them as real.

Let's dive into the power of setting intentions.

> Living with intention stops your stupid.
> Our intention creates our reality.
>
> —Wayne Dyer

The dictionary describes *intention* as an act or instance of determining mentally upon some action or result. It is also defined as an aim or a plan. As I have emphasized, what you think about is what you will speak about, and this is what you will bring about—so think wisely, my friend. Having a clear target or intention to aim for and think about will allow you to enjoy the life you desire and reach your goals.

Keep your thoughts and aim steady through focusing. The intention on staying focused keeps you from being reactive and from getting stuck in a never-ending loop of ups and downs and knee-jerk reactions. When you embark on creating a better life for yourself, you will focus on what you want, and this will be positive for you. It will allow your higher self to use your guidance systems and give you clear direction. This will springboard you into the life you truly desire.

Sometimes it takes a negative event to get us to focus. It can be easy to fall back into old patterns because they are familiar. When this happens, instead of furthering your life, it sets you back. Remember that there is no wrong choice. There is only furthering your path. When you experience something negative, there is an equal and opposite feeling that is positive. This new, stronger, positive thought and feeling becomes your new set point for that which you are striving.

For instance, I would sometimes get complacent and slowly stop doing what worked, like educating my patients regularly. Whenever I did that, however, my number of patient visits dropped, and so did my income. I also got fewer new referrals, which meant less business, which meant that by the time I received checks from the insurance companies, I found myself in a financial pinch. And when that happened, it reminded me that falling short on what works, like continued education for every patient, always catches up with me.

Living this way is not okay; my staff depends on me to drive the business. You likely can relate. For instance, you may have felt great when you kept to your health regimens, but when you fell off, it woke you up to the fact that you didn't feel as good. We often unconsciously fall back to the familiar, which isn't always our best option. Initially, as this happens, it can cause an emotional setback that seems like a really big deal. Once you have a good understanding of the process of creation and allowing, your outlook and reaction will change.

When you fall back into old patterns, you can quickly recognize the negativity. This will allow you to refocus quickly and restart your positive direction by following the RGS and EGS. Instead of being upset that you lost track, you will be excited that you caught yourself and can change direction before the momentum builds.

Remember that you always have a choice between heading toward your goals and accomplishments and distracting yourself with the familiar, which will lead you astray from your deepest desires. The first step to the good life of health, wealth, and love is always getting clear on your intentions. This will bring you happiness. When you are clear on your intentions, the thoughts you receive from your EGS and RGS will show you the best and fastest way to get the results you desire.

One action I take daily is to look at photos, written affirmations, and my lists of goals that I have on my wall. I find that photos and affirmations light up and direct my EGS to take me where I want to go. For example, I had large photos, from brochures I picked up at car dealers, of a white Range Rover and a black Escalade on my wall for years. I am happy to report I now have them both in my garage.

I created a board of photos of all my desires and then focused on the feeling of attaining my desires and reaching my goals. I found that when I was too much in my head and trying to figure out where to go and how to get there, I often got lost, tired, and unfocused.

There is a secret, however, that all the most successful people use, and I will reveal that to you shortly. You can have everything you want, easily and effortlessly, if you will listen to your inner GPS—your guidance system.

Imagine wanting to travel to another state but you refuse to use a map. A map or guidance system will allow you to look over long distances, but refusing that will only allow you to see what is right in front of you. A map may take you around a lake or to a bridge to cross a river, but without that direction you will walk straight into an obstacle, and it may take longer to find your destination. Paying attention to your feelings means you're following your guidance system to get you where you want to go.

The secret to getting what you want, easily and effortlessly, is to do work only after you are inspired to take an action. This is what I mean by following your guidance system. People often seem to talk about effort and hard work. And for some people that will work, but most of us get tired and give up before we get the results. Then we just say that it's not meant to be, or it's too hard, or that other people are just lucky or smarter. The hardest work is staying focused and feeling the results and then waiting for inspired action. Work led by inspiration is fun and exciting. At times, it may even seem hard, but inspired action is work that is fun, effortless, and rewarding. Work without inspiration takes effort.

At times, my desires change, and so will yours. This is okay and normal. I took those desires off my picture board, like the saltwater fish tank I realized I didn't want to clean and maintain. On the other hand, I stared daily at the most important items, like the car I wanted to drive, and it is now in my garage. Any desire can be achieved just as easily. A button is as easy to create as a castle. It just depends on your ability to believe and feel it happening.

Take a few moments and visualize what you will put on your own board of intentions. Feel how it might be to drive the car of your dreams or have the relationship you daydream of being in—the more specific the better. Claim whatever you feel as real, and your emotional guidance system will lead you toward that dream.

How to Program Your EGS to Get You to Where You Want to Go

First, you must fully understand the law of attraction. You get what you think about, no matter if you want it or not. The universe and the law of attraction does not hear the word no. If you say to yourself, "I do not want to be poor anymore," the universe will give you more of the poorness. When you say, "I want to be wealthy [or financially free and abundant]," the universe will give you that. Many of us try manifesting using negative emotions, guided by our stupid reactions; we try to push through or force life to change. Or we feel there are limitations in the universe, and someone has what we want, or we take something away from others. That kind of thinking allows those exact people and manifestations into our lives and pushes away our desires. Our negative emotions will control our actions and our guidance systems, keeping our intentions from being brought to fruition. When you choose to listen to your higher self, however, the thoughts you receive will give you inspiration and guide you in the best direction, attracting the perfect people and desires to you.

In the writing, editing, and production of this book, when I set small intentions through focusing on limiting, stupid thoughts, my goals were small—and nothing happened. Then, when I focused on creating a best-selling book that could reach and help many people, a former mentor of mine, who has written nonfiction best-sellers, called to wish me happy holidays. Weeks later, he and I met to discuss and outline my plan for producing my book, as well as added-value products and a marketing plan. When I shifted from my stupid thinking to my smart thinking, he showed up!

Living with intention, with clear goals to aim for, will constantly take you closer to your goal. Listening to your EGS will light up the path to get you there. Remember it's not like the old paradigm of forced action; instead, it's trusting that the universe wants to hear from you and deliver what you desire. Forced action takes you off the path and on hurtful and costly detours, whereas trusting and listening to your EGS brings your desires to you in a much easier way. Sometimes, it even feels like a miracle! I believe that my higher self already sees the best picture for my life, as it has been defined by the contrast I have lived up until now. It's up to me to trust the path my EGS and RGS direct me toward.

We are hardwired to attract what we want by the law of attraction. First, we live some contrast, and then we create desires. Then our desires are created by our higher selves, and when we are ready, we receive them. We live through attraction, not resistance or assertion. Nothing asserts itself into our lives.

Understanding the law of attraction means taking responsibility for everything in your life and saying, "I did that." Your thoughts attract things, situations, and daily life to you. If it is happening, no matter how good or bad, you created it and allowed it into your life—no exceptions. Things are not forced on you. There is only the allowing of things you want or disallowing them by resisting them and allowing the negative in.

Whatever you spend your time thinking about will find you. We are not pawns on a chessboard, randomly moved around; we are not pinballs in a game. Once we realize that our thoughts create the board, we become the directors of every move we make.

Whenever I tried to force my business to grow by making myself call the same list of people over and over, it didn't work. I didn't trust that my patients would come if I offered that which would serve their highest good. I found that trying too hard or forcing needed products and supplements on patients lost me some business, even though I had the best intentions of helping more people. I was working hard and stupid, not being inspired and smart.

You Receive Thoughts Each Moment from Your Higher Self

The way you think about the situations in your life are based on your dominant thoughts. Dominant thoughts that affect your response to life are influenced by all your former thoughts to previous situations. This is why you react and feel as you do about your current life. This is how your belief system is made. A belief is just a thought that has been repeated over and over until you feel it is always true. The *Merriam-Webster Dictionary* defines a belief as "an acceptance that a statement is true or that something exists." Just because you believe it doesn't mean it's true.

When you meditate and focus on the positive, you tap in to your higher self. Tapping in or connecting will allow you to receive thoughts from your higher self or guidance systems. You may believe that you know the best route to take because you have been there many times, but the car's GPS knows a better way because of its perspective of all roads. When you think about a dream, intention, or inspiration, you may wonder where it is coming from. It's a thought received from your higher self.

In your past, you may have had big dreams that didn't come to fruition, and you may have wondered where those dreams came from and why they didn't come true. Your dreams and desires always come from life experiences. They are born of contrast. If they have not come to reality yet, it is because, in some way, you are not allowing them to do so. Your desires are ready for you, and they are there; you, however, are not ready to receive them yet.

If you are in Ohio and want to be in Florida, you start your trip, but you don't get mad when you're only in Georgia. You understand that you are on your way, and you will get there. The same is true with your desires. When you set your intentions, never doubt what your EGS and RGS are showing you; just keep following their guidance through inspiration. If you have dreams, they are 100 percent the best path to take.

Let's do an exercise to help you gain clarity about the intentions you set.

1. What is one aspect of your life (health, wealth, or love) that you thought was negative and you desired to change for the better?
2. What did you do to improve it?
3. How did you feel, once you improved it?
4. What was at least one positive aspect that came from that change?

For question 1, everyone has at least one aspect—whether it's health, wealth, or love—that is dominant and one that is not. For example, you may be rich but struggle with attracting your love partner. You may be very consistent with maintaining your health but are challenged by managing your finances.

I invite you to go back to the intentions you set above and determine which ones you are smartest at obtaining and which you are the stupidest at attracting into your life. It's key to know in which areas you are strongest or more dominant when creating the life you desire.

Rank health, wealth, and love, from your smartest to stupidest.

1.
2.
3.

The purpose of the making the above lists is to give you hope and confidence. You likely are smart in one area, but by the time you finish this book, you will be smarter in all three.

We all have gone through challenges and will continue to face challenges throughout our lives. When you act with your stupid mind, you react negatively to challenges and see them as bad things. When you use your smart mind, however, you know that challenges offer clarity and opportunity. You may underestimate your power to set intentions and realize them. It's amazing to see your intentions and desires come to reality. You need to have clarity before you make any decisions, and clarity comes from being in tune with your guidance systems. Your guidance systems will take you down the path of least resistance, which will get you where you want to go faster.

On a side note, remember that there are no wrong decisions, and no matter what, you can always tune in again to your guidance systems. You will then be redirected to where you want to go with the least resistance.

Often, when we have negative experiences or negative emotions, we want to force a change in our physical reality. If we need more money, we try to find a way to work harder or get another job. Believe it or not, that is a backward approach. First, we must change our reactions and negative emotions into positive emotions. We must pivot. For example, sometimes being on the path of least resistance means staying at a job that we feel underpays us and is restrictive, while we desire to be paid more and enjoy extra freedom.

Do not make a decision until you have clarity from your guidance system. You may be ready to take a leap, but maybe the leap is not the path of least resistance. Taking action without clarity, guidance, and inspiration is stupid and will lead only to negative results. Maybe you need to learn to change your feeling and appreciate where you are before inspiration will hit you. Your higher self does not want you to keep repeating the same problem over and over. You may not make a move to improve that situation, or you may move to soon, but if you stop to actively listen to your EGS, it will be in your ear, guiding you to better feelings about the situation and, eventually, to the type of employment that will meet all your needs. You might even be surprised that it can happen right where you are.

When you don't listen to your EGS, on the other hand, you most likely will keep repeating the same actions and getting the same types of employment, over and over.

Moving with Intention versus Reacting Unconsciously

Your dominant thoughts from the past—your beliefs—create your current reality; they will create your future reality and changed beliefs. If you consistently watch negative news on TV, your focus on your current reality will be influenced by what you watched. Sadly, that can make you afraid and more reactive, and it can take you further from your EGS. The RGS will filter in the things that you think about and to which you pay attention.

After watching negative news one evening and continuing to think about those things, the next day you might find that at work you are exposed to people who reinforce that negative news and thinking. You're allowing and creating reactive talking and knee-jerk emotions based on fictitious things. For many of us, it is easier to see or believe what is around us because we can physically touch, see, taste, and smell it, and that is our only reality. What actually happens is that our thoughts, created from past experiences, create our current thoughts and emotions.

When things are not as we want them to be, it is because we created them and then allowed them into our lives by reaction, not intention. Living with intention means taking responsibility for our lives and everything we create—the good and the bad. Taking responsibility for all you create in life will put you in the driver's seat and create a new type of freedom for you.

This is where living with intention becomes important because when it all comes down to it, we are trying to get more of what we desire because we think that will make us feel better.

Living with intention means creating the feeling of it before you see it, which will then bring your desires to fruition. This will help you create more of what you want.

Living in Contrast

Sometimes, life shows us what we *don't* want; it's as simple as that. None of us consciously intends to live a worse life or to be sick or poor or stupid. When we live without intention, however, that is exactly what happens. My suggestion is to use contrast as your ally. Once you find out what you *don't* want, you can consciously think about the opposite, which is what you *do* want. Then it's up to you to focus with intention and allow your guidance systems to show you the directions.

The next step is to imagine what it would feel like to have what you desire. Think of your best life. It's always up to you. You can create it—or you can keep it away. Intend to have better love, wealth, health, and happiness in your life, and it will manifest. For example, if you want a new car, first you need to decide which car you want. Put all your focus on the type of car you desire. Include all the details! Then imagine how it will feel to own that car. What would it feel like to hear the sound of starting the engine? What would the seats feel like? These feelings are the precursors to the creations. Remember that what you want becomes real when you believe you will feel better by having it and that you deserve it.

The truth is, you need to own the feeling first. Once you do—and you hold on to that feeling—the momentum will build, and it will happen!

This can apply to anything in your life. This is called living with intention. By living or experiencing something that you *do not* want and then knowing what you *do* want, you give yourself the chance to live each moment and make each decision in life based on where you want to go, not where you've been. The only reason you want to go there is because of how it will make you feel. Once you understand that, you will understand that seeing isn't believing, but believing will lead you to seeing.

Fixing your stupid allows all parts of the good life to work together. Remember what I keep saying: there are three parts to everyone's good life—health, wealth, and love. This is the balance of true happiness.

Most people want to live a better version of life, no matter where they are in life. I sense that because you are reading this book, that includes you too. It's great if you seek to be happier in love, healthier, and wealthier. Anything you desire always falls into one of those three categories. Think of anything you want in life—it's because you think it will make you happier in love, healthier, or wealthier. And when you break it down, you want to be healthier or wealthier or more in love only because you think it will make you happier.

Again, that's why I wrote this book. I discovered that fixing your stupid with intention allows you to be more aligned with your spirit or higher self—your guide to the life you want. On the other hand, feeding your stupid will make you spend more time reacting; more time calling or allowing what you don't want. Here's the bottom line: your reactions will create situations that only get bigger and bigger. You will stay in the same place in life, repeating the same things over and over.

Fixing your stupid, however, allows you to step outside that repetitive circle and move on to the next level.

Remember that whenever you leave a situation, you take yourself to the next level. Don't fall back down a level by looking in your rearview mirror and focusing on what is back there. Also remember that there is no end to the stairway you are on, and that's okay. It does not mean that you aren't happy or satisfied. Experience will always lead to new desires and new parts of your stupid to fix so you can get to those desires. You can talk yourself up or talk yourself down. It's always up to you.

Always Remember: Our Stupid Builds Momentum

Little hinges swing big doors.

—Dr. Fred Schofield, DC

The thoughts and actions you have will add momentum to your life. Momentum goes either in the direction you want to go or in the opposite direction. Momentum means that the bigger it gets, the bigger it gets, and the harder it is to turn around. This goes for positive or negative actions. Small momentum is easy to change before it gets going too much and becomes hard to stop. A cruise ship is much harder to turn around than a ski boat. A car at the top of a hill is easy to stop in the first few seconds after it begins to roll, but once the car builds up speed, it gets harder and harder to stop.

It is possible to change direction, however, no matter how much momentum you have. It just takes more time, and sometimes it takes letting life situations play out. Don't be tricked; if you let it, your stupid mind will tell you that intense momentum is impossible to stop and that you shouldn't even try. Listen to your higher self, and you will be guided to the best way to stop the momentum of movement in a negative direction. Momentum also moves in a positive direction, and you can add momentum to live your life in a more positive way.

If everything we want in life happens because we think that it will make us happier, why do we sometimes do what we do to stop it? Why do we not let the good momentum build? Why do we eat that extra doughnut when we think that being skinny will make us happy? We do it because that doughnut makes us happy in the moment. The same applies when we buy that extra shirt we can't afford. It's immediate gratification.

We think that shirt and doughnut will make us happier, but these are short-term items that makes us happy only in the moment. Sometimes, we listen to our stupid minds and feel that we cannot reach our long-term goals, so we just choose immediate gratification. Then we beat ourselves up for what we have done. In many cases, we give up on what we want, feeling it's impossible or too late for us. This causes us to become unhappy, and our momentum builds in the wrong direction, making it that much harder to get what we want.

Remember, you only want what you want because you think you will feel better once you have it. It's always up to you to feed the wolf. I recommend you feed the smart one!

1. Name one intention for each area of happiness: health, wealth, and love.

    _____

    _____

    _____

2. Name one instance in which you have strong positive momentum and how it is affecting your life.

    _____

    _____

    _____

3. Name one instance in which you have strong negative momentum and what you can do to change it.

_____

_____

_____

4. Affirmations and Visualizations

I am moving forward, building momentum in the direction I want to go, and understanding that my guidance gives me peace and confidence.
I achieve my goals regardless of external influences.
I am on a path that is leading me to where I want to go.

CHAPTER 9

Staying Smart with Regular Maintenance

Success is never final; failure is never fatal. It's courage that counts.

—John Wooden

LET'S FACE IT: IN TODAY'S BUSY, MOTIVATED, HIGH-TECH world, we are thinking during most of our waking hours. In fact, according to the Laboratory of Neuro Imaging at the University of Southern California, the average person has about 48.6 thoughts per minute, which means we most likely have, on average, seventy thousand thoughts per day.

I'm not suggesting that you should stop thinking or that you're thinking too much; just the opposite. My recommendation is that since you will be thinking anyway, be aware of, focus on, and direct which thoughts you let enter and stay in your head. I call this *focused thinking*, rather than scattered thinking. In this chapter, you will see the power of harnessing your thoughts to direct and guide you.

Hunters tell me if they shoot their shotguns in the direction of a flock of flying birds, they never hit one. They describe it as blasting pellets from their shotgun carelessly into the air, with no specific aim. (Maybe that's where the term *shotgun approach* comes from.) However, if you aim at one bird in the flock, you will hit one almost every time.

It's the same with your thinking. If you blast out a bunch of scattered thoughts, who knows where they will take you? Most likely, you will just keep thinking random, stupid thoughts; worry about something; and then spin out control by thinking up fictional problems and negative outcomes. Have you ever had an argument in your head before you even got into an upcoming situation? This is negative or stupid thinking. This is creating negative outcomes. You will keep reacting to your current reality instead of taking action and continually creating a better one.

Focused thinking, on the other hand, helps you be more specific and more positive with your thinking, especially when it comes to manifesting what you desire. You will aim for your target and direct your thinking to hit the bull's-eye.

For instance, when you have a thought that you want more money, what does that really mean? What will more money allow you to have? Is it freedom? Time? More stuff? Cars? More relationships? Be very specific on what you want and why. Are you saying you want an extra dollar an hour in wages or to win the $100 million lottery? In Tim Ferriss's book, *The 4-Hour Work Week*, he gives a "dreamline" to help people focus on what they want, specifically, with action steps. This is a great example of focused thinking. There also are emotional undercurrents and a sense of purpose you may be missing out on when you have unfocused, stupid thoughts. Focused thinking takes into consideration the question of why you want more money and what emotions are driving this train of thinking. Your smart thinking will know that money may satisfy you for a short time, but you will then just move on to another want or desire because you don't appreciate that feeling of what you created and manifested by having more money.

I keep going back to the fact that you want what you want because of the feeling you think you will get by having it. If you push through and force things to happen without changing the feeling first, the newness will wear off, and you will move on to the next thing to feel better. That's not a bad thing, but it is a little stupid when it comes to living the good life. What if you could achieve the feeling that you desire by just thinking and then knowing you will have it?

This is where a lot of people get confused. I don't want you to *not* get what you want. I'm saying that you might think feeling good *without* the manifestation might stop it from coming, but once you feel the feeling and allow that to be enough, you will not be able to stop the manifestations from happening. I will say again that *believing is seeing*, not the other way around.

Appreciate the manifestation by starting with appreciating your desire. Next, feel the emotion as it unfolds. After all, you come for the creating, not for the creation. What if you could start your thoughts with that feeling, even before you earn the money? It would make the manifestation so much sweeter—and it would happen so much faster. What if you could appreciate every little step as it unfolds in the creation? You don't want all the food you will ever eat in front of you right now. After all, it's all about manifesting, not the manifestation.

It's not what you have done by the end of your life that matters; how you felt and your experiences during your life are what matters.

The good feeling—the rush—that we are looking for is in the creation. Isn't the best part of buying a car the test drive, the final choice, and then actually bringing it home? For a few days, it's really exciting to see it each morning in your driveway or garage. It isn't long, however, before that your excitement wears off, and then you lose that feeling and start looking toward something else. There is nothing wrong with that. I just want you to see that it is about the manifesting, not the manifestation. Holding the feeling of manifesting takes focused, smart thinking. This allows you to feel good every day, no matter what; then more manifesting can happen. Smart, focused thinking connects your thoughts and feelings to create the manifestations that you desire. It's the feeling you desire, not the goal itself.

A Short Exercise to Experience What I'm Talking About

Recall a time when something excited you so much that you felt goosebumps on your skin. Feel that feeling again now. Think back to when you got your first bike. What color was the bike, and how did it feel when you first rode it? Think back to when you got your first car. What color was the car, and how did it feel when you first drove it?

Those feelings you just felt are always alive in you. With focused thinking, you can *always* inspire those types of feelings when you envision your desires, and they will help you manifest them.

Each time you use focused thinking, it's an opportunity to create even more manifestations. This is such an important lesson to understand.

The Focused-Thinking Thirty-Day Plan

To change your habits and maintain a life of focused thinking, I'm asking you to follow my thirty-day plan, which can take from thirty to sixty minutes per day. You may wonder why I chose thirty days. When NASA did a study with astronauts, they found that it took twenty-five to thirty days for the subconscious mind to learn new habits and for those habits to be neurologically ingrained in the body and mind.

They test-tracked and measured astronauts to see how they responded to being upside down in space, without gravity. The astronauts wore special goggles that made the world look upside down. After twenty-five to thirty days, each astronaut began to see the world right-side up. Their brains had created fresh neural pathways. NASA concluded that it took an uninterrupted period of up to thirty days to reprogram the unconscious mind and develop a new habit.

In a study released in the *European Journal of Social Psychology*, Phillippa Lally and her team of researchers surveyed ninety-six people over a twelve-week period to discover how long it would take to drop an old habit and start a new one. Over the twelve weeks, the participants chose a new habit. At the end of the period, Lally found the average time it took for the participants to pick up a new habit was sixty-six days.

Some habitual patterns of thinking may resist focused thinking and take longer. Either way, try the plan below for thirty days, minimum, and notice your thoughts to see if they become more focused. See if your emotional state has changed to be more positive and what manifestations have taken place.

When I first put this plan together, it took me several restarts of the plan to get through it. But each time I learned something, and my desires grew stronger, as did my resolve.

I also noticed that at each restart, the positive results started coming faster. This was very exciting.

Of course, every human is different, with his or her own unique patterns and blocks to change. I suggest trying the following plan for a minimum of thirty days; then notice how much you succeeded in adapting to more focused thinking. Changing the pattern of how you respond to your thoughts can free you of the unconscious—and many times, detrimental—thinking patterns that get in the way of your manifesting what you desire. You have the power to change your thinking. You have the power to fix your stupid! You have the power to be smart!

Changing My Thinking Pattern

> We cannot solve our problems with the same thinking we used when we created them.
>
> —Albert Einstein

The plan I will share with you comes from my own desire to change my unfocused thoughts with regard to wealth and earning money. My stupid thinking got in my way. I always had a job and would earn, make, or seem to manifest "just enough" money. I could never let myself hold focus long enough to determine what I truly wanted, financially. I saw colleagues and friends to whom money came easily and who seemed to manage it effortlessly.

Realizing that my weakest link was wealth, I immersed myself in a variety of self-improvement seminars and trainings. I read books and bought courses to learn more about becoming abundant and how to change the beliefs that were holding me back from having an overflow of money.

I was always able to earn money, yet I spent it on the wrong things and didn't plan well. I knew I had to change some of my habits, as they were keeping me on edge every month when the bills came. The first thing I did was make a vision board. As I mentioned earlier, my vision board had photos showing the kind of wealth I deserved. I knew that looking at my wealth vision board daily would bring me closer to what I desired and deserved in my business and personal life. My board contained not just "things" but experiences in all three areas too. Looking at the board helped me focus on my deepest desires and feel what it would be like to have these things in my life. This helped me program my emotion and reticular guidance systems.

As with anything new, it was only a short time before I got stupid and stopped looking at my board every day, and then my momentum fell off. I recommitted and got back on the horse. I looked at it every day for ten minutes. It worked! It took me about two days to feel the shift and about four days to see manifestations materializing.

In about a month, I felt a greater sense of self-confidence from looking at my visions and feeling the emotions they invoked in me—and my income increased. Yet even though I knew more of what I wanted when it came to money, I knew inside that, ultimately, I still had to tackle my inherited beliefs about money.

My main teacher about money was my mom, who always had just enough money to get us by. She worked for a wage, and when the check arrived, her wagon filled up, but before the next one arrived, her wagon was empty. I learned that when it came to money, you earn what you need and spend it; then you wait for your next paycheck before you can buy anything else.

My father was the same way. My family handed me a belief: "Work hard, live paycheck to paycheck, and have just enough to get by." No thanks.

That was the area I focused on changing within me for several months. I was 100 percent committed to fixing my stupid, so I immersed myself in changing my inherited beliefs in private, body-centered therapy sessions and seminars with some of the biggest names in the self-help arena. One book I discovered in my journey was *Rich Dad Poor Dad* (1997) by Robert Kiyosaki. I could relate fully when I read,

> One dad had a habit of saying, "I can't afford it."
> The other dad forbade those words to be used.
> He insisted that I ask, "How can I afford it?"
> One is a statement and the other is a question.
> One lets you off the hook and the other forces
> you to think.

Wow, that gave me a realization that I was not using my smart mind and asking the right questions. I was using my stupid mind to make statements like, "I can afford that," or "I'll just work harder and make more money." Yes, I was being positive, but it was stupidly positive. It wasn't until I started asking myself questions and then listening to my guidance system for answers that I truly began to expand my thoughts and ideas and my focused thinking.

What Will Be Your Focus for the Next Thirty Days?

You might have focused thoughts that create success in some areas of your life, while in other areas, you may be unfocused and unaware of how scattered your thinking is. My challenge was changing my beliefs around earning and managing money. Yours could be about discovering and changing beliefs that blindside you when it comes to love. Or perhaps you feel stupid when it comes to maintaining your health.

Remember that a huge part of your current reality in every area of your life is a result of your past. We all learned belief systems from others that affect our decisions and feelings in our lives. Your guidance system may need some tough love from you. Help steer it in the most beneficial direction to get you the best results from doing your daily ritual. Don't wait to have several wake-up calls, like I did, before you finally change your stupid thinking and create an overflow of wealth in your life. If you are at a breaking point, then jump in *now*—full blast. What are you willing to do to get what you want? This may seem like a silly question, but most people don't take such a question seriously—and that's why so many people are stuck in stupid cycles.

For me, it got real when I had five growing children who needed more clothes, food, and a hundred other things. I had to make a plan and follow it. I also looked at my spending patterns. I had just purchased a new x-ray machine for my office when a hurricane hit, and we were closed for an entire month. On top of no income, some patients demanded refunds for their prepaid plans with me. I was stupid, as I hadn't saved for emergencies, just like my parents hadn't. I still had to pay seven thousand dollars in office rent, and my kids still needed food and clothing. That woke me up, big time. I needed to change my reality. I knew I had to pull myself up by my bootstraps and apply all that I had learned in books, therapy, and seminars.

I poured through notes and videos and decided to pick the best components of what I had learned. I created a ritual and a plan to manifest specific, long-term financial results for me, my patients, and my family. I thought, *I can't control the weather, but I surely can change my beliefs and patterns when it came to managing money.* I finally understood the question—what was I willing to do to get what I wanted? I went into inspired hyper-focus mode and created a daily routine to follow, which included nine actions. I committed to doing this every single day of my life, no matter what. More than anything, I knew I wanted to feel better. I committed to feeling better about money, no matter the physical outcome. Even if I had money in the bank, I always had felt anxious. I knew that was the cycle I created over and over, except I had always blamed it on the outside world.

I knew that to change my patterns and make a real momentum shift, I needed to practice what my teachers had taught me. To change my outcome and my feelings, I had to change my belief. After all, a belief is only a feeling that has repeated itself in your life, over and over, until you believe it to be true. The definition of belief, according to the *Merriam-Webster Dictionary*, is "an acceptance that a statement is true or that something exists." That doesn't necessarily mean that what you believe is true.

Now that you understand that some of your beliefs are fact and others fiction, you will be able to let go of the ones that are holding you back.

Where Beliefs Hold You Back

> The truth is there is no actual stress or anxiety in the world; it's your thoughts that create these false beliefs.
>
> —Wayne Dyer

I pulled the best of what I had learned about affirmations from Dr. Fred Scofield. I went back and scanned the best meditations that I had learned from Abraham Hicks. I spent time in Hawaii, working with Steve Sisgold on changing my beliefs. I read the 2017 book *Make Your Bed* by William H. McRaven, who said,

> If you want to change the world, start off by making your bed. Nothing can replace the strength and comfort of one's faith, but sometimes the simple act of making your bed can give you the lift you need to start your day and provide you the satisfaction to end it right.

The simple habit of making my bed in the morning changed the way I felt—I felt like I was accomplishing something. Doing my morning ritual began to carry over into the rest of my day. Not only did I feel better, but I also started to attract more money within weeks of starting the ritual. When I went to my bank, they told me about an account I'd forgot about—with over five thousand dollars in it! I was so stupid about money that I'd forgotten I had opened that years before.

I also began managing my money in smarter ways. Overall, I felt more connected to my EGS and my innate wisdom. My reticular guidance system showed me opportunities that I couldn't see before. Doing my morning ritual continued to reinforce within me a focus that forever boosted my health, wealth, and love. Happiness through balance never had felt so good! I was finally living the good life.

You Are Becoming the Person You Want to Be

Like a butterfly, you can change and spread your wings each day. The ultimate version of you is within you already. A caterpillar and a butterfly are the same insect in a different version. Always remember that you, like the caterpillar, can create your reality with each emotion and decision that you make and become a butterfly as a result. Doing the daily ritual plan will remind you that you have ultimate freedom and power to change stupid thoughts to smart ones. You hold the key to whatever you want to create—now. The plan I have put together will help you easily live and think your way to a smarter and more successful life.

And like all plans, don't be hard on yourself if you have ups and downs while doing it. This plan is not about you doing it perfectly; no one is grading you. There are parts of life where changing your thinking habits will be easy and parts that you will find hard. This is the same for all of us.

While my thinking about money was always stressful, thoughts about forging relationships were easy. I always felt comfortable around anyone. People seemed to almost always like me. When I was in high school, I was friends with most people. One of my good friends and I were talking in school one day, and she told me that she thought of me as a Renaissance man—I seemed to know a little about everything and could relate to anyone.

When it came to my health, I always had good thoughts. I was able to gain or lose weight without much thought or stress, and if I felt under the weather, I knew that I was stressing out my body's immune system, so my thinking was clear and focused. I knew to rest and take some vitamins, and I was confident I would get better quickly. My Achilles' heel was my relationship with money.

If you look at your life, you will see similar ups and downs in different parts of your thinking, about either your health, wealth, or love. The plan I will present to you will help you focus your thinking where you need it the most. As you follow my plan, I suggest you evaluate where you are today and where you want to go, and adjust your daily thinking to reflect the new you.

Creating Your Morning Ritual

I do nine components every day to manifest quickly what I desire in my life. I have been doing this every day for several years. Try it for thirty days; hopefully, it will become a daily routine for the rest of your life—because it works! To stay smart in your thinking, you must have a focused morning routine. Starting the day off right is the most important thing you can do. It is a set point for what you will attract or allow into your life for that day. Each day will build momentum.

Choose to make each day of your life special. Stop living for the weekend or the next holiday or vacation. Make every day count. When I started doing this, it made my life happier and more consistent. This is when I realized that every day was an opportunity that I created.

As I developed this routine, I realized that my emotions were tied to the days of the week. For instance, I had programmed myself to be happier on Fridays because that was the last workday of the week. On Sunday, I felt blue, as the weekend was ending. I even focused on Wednesday as "hump day," putting in my brain that I was only days away from the happier weekend mood. I was a slave to the calendar, and this was not helpful to my emotional state or my abundant thinking. It was actually very self-limiting.

I felt different, depending on the day of the week, and I knew I had to stop this pattern. I did so by creating my morning ritual and setting the tone for every day, which started with intention. Very quickly, each day started feeling the same.

It was like starting each day on a trampoline with a bounce before I left my house. It's up to you, but I like to listen to music while I do my morning ritual. I listen to baroque-style music, such as Mozart, as I feel it helps me raise my vibration. You can find baroque music on Apple Music, Amazon Music, or Pandora apps. I chose this type of music after reading a book called *The Mozart Effect* by Don Campbell. He condensed the world's research on all the beneficial effects of certain types of music. His book discusses a study that reveals how music makes you smarter. Major corporations, such as Shell, IBM, and DuPont, along with hundreds of schools and universities, use music, such as certain baroque and "Mozart effect" pieces, to cut learning time in half and increase retention of the new materials.

A few of the hundreds of benefits of the Mozart effect that Campbell shares include the following:

- It improves test scores.
- It cuts learning time.
- It calms hyperactive children and adults.
- It reduces errors.
- It improves creativity and clarity.
- It heals the body faster.
- It integrates both sides of the brain for more efficient learning.
- It raises IQ scores nine points.
  (Research done at University of California, Irvine)

The Focused-Thinking Thirty-Day Plan

1. Waking (fifteen minutes, maximum)

I suggest you wake up every day at the same time, even on days off from work or school. I get up at five o'clock daily. This may be hard for some of you. I know that getting up on Saturday morning at five o'clock may not sound fun or smart to you, but it gives you control of your life. Think of it like this: Did you ever wake up early on the weekend because you were going to do something fun? Maybe you were going on a fishing or hunting trip, or you had an early tee time on the golf course or an early flight for a vacation. That made it easy for you to get up early—and to be excited too, right?

Now, set a time to get up each day and know you get to choose how you feel about each day's events. Choose the feeling of the best day you could have. Then wake up and focus on feeling that way. Here's what I do: I set my alarm to go off fifteen minutes before I plan to get out of bed. Initially, I had to put my alarm across the room to ensure that I didn't hit the snooze button over and over—that helped me to get this process started. I recommend you move your alarm away from your bed so you will have to get out of bed to turn it off.

2. Appreciation (one to five minutes)

Once your alarm goes off, focus your mind by spending a few minutes in appreciation.

A surefire way to stop your stupid mind from lying in bed, creating drama over problems, is to focus on appreciating all you do and have now. It gets rid of the morning blues and engages your mind with positive thoughts. Initially, your stupid, negative mind can set a bad tone for your day, but it's always a choice. You could lie there feeling angry about being up so early or how sleepy you feel, or you could feel blessed to be alive another day. Appreciate any and all things in your life as the first thing you do.

It could start with how much you like your bed or your soft pillow. Then you can ramp it up to the many blessings in your life and the opportunities you have that day. The key is to start small and build momentum on the things you appreciate. It's easier to feel good about general things, but as your momentum builds, you can get more specific without overthinking it. Then end that step by appreciating the things that are coming to you. Be thankful for the desires you want to create, and affirm that they are on their way.

3. Connecting (one to five minutes)

Once I have fully appreciated what I have and what I will have, I move to step 3: connecting. No matter what you believe in, you need to connect to it. It's like plugging in the toaster before you use it. A toaster without power will not toast your bread.

You will get so much more done with less effort when you plug in to your power.

This may be focusing on your God or spirit. It could be your spirit guide or someone who has passed on. No matter what you believe in, focus on it to amp up your day. When you plug in to this power, it will be like turning on the GPS to take you wherever you want to go that day. You will be well on your way to making your visions a reality.

4. Affirmations

By now, you've noticed that every chapter ends with affirmations—those short, focused sentences aimed at affecting the conscious and subconscious mind. Repeating the short, positive statements will start your day smarter. The words of the affirmation will bring up related mental images in your mind, automatically and involuntarily. You will become that better version of yourself in your mind, which will inspire, energize, and motivate you. Repeating affirmations and seeing the resultant mental images affect the subconscious mind, which in turn influences your behavior, choices, habits, actions, and reactions.

Here's what affirmations do:

- They motivate.
- They keep the mind focused on the goal.
- They influence the subconscious mind and activate its powers.
- They change the way you think and behave. This will bring you into contact with new people to help you with your goals.
- They make you feel positive, energetic, and active, and, therefore, they put you in a better position to transform your inner and external worlds.

To help you keep track, use apps on your phone or use rosary or mala beads to help you count out your affirmations. Choose a simple affirmation that resonates with you today. Repeat each affirmation 108 times. You might remember from the introduction why I chose the number 108—it's considered sacred in many Eastern religions, such as Hinduism, Buddhism, Jainism, and Sikhism, and other traditions, like connected yoga-based practices. The prehistoric monument Stonehenge is 108 feet in diameter. It is no surprise that the early Vedic sages were renowned mathematicians—in fact, they invented our number system. A mala and a rosary are each composed of 108 beads.

I figured all those different cultures must know something, so I do my affirmations 108 times, and I count them using mala beads.

Some of my first affirmations were "I am getting happier," "I am excited for what is coming," and "I create my reality."

If this is new to you, remember that it takes time to get used to new habits. One day of saying affirmations is not enough. The power of repetition affects your ability to attract and call in what you want. It is just a piece of the puzzle in changing unfocused, stupid thinking to focused, smart thinking. Each piece of the puzzle is part of the entire picture—and the whole is greater than the sum of its parts. Take a minute to truly grasp that concept.

5. Make Your Bed (three to five minutes)

As previously mentioned, follow Admiral McRafen's advice: "If you want to make a difference in the world, start by making your bed." This may sound silly, but it works! For years, I never made my bed. I thought, *Why should I? I am a grown adult, and I am just going to get back in the bed tonight.* But just as with repeating the affirmations and getting up at the same time each day, making my bed helped me feel in control of my life.

It's another small thing that keeps order in your life. This will translate to how you act and feel as you move out into the world during your day. Also, if a day of contrast or negativity plays out, at least you will have a clean room and made bed to get into at night.

6. Journaling (three to five minutes)

It is very important to write things down daily. Michael LeBoeuf, author of *The Millionaire in You* (2002), says, "When you write down your ideas you automatically focus your full attention on them." Few of us can write one thought and think about another thought at the same time. Thus, a pencil and paper make excellent concentration tools.

When I first heard about journaling and decided to try it, I felt great getting things out of my head and on to paper. I intended to fill up a full page every day. Some days I could write easily, but on other days, it was tough and took me a long time to get through it, which was why I eventually stopped. To prevent that from happening to you, I suggest you write a minimum of one sentence daily—yes, *just one*. This will make your journaling easy to complete, even on the hardest days. If you miss a day, you can easily catch up. Write at least one sentence about how you are feeling each day and how you want the day to go. It can be anything you are inspired to write down.

7. Vision Board (three to five minutes)

Author Jack Canfield's blog says this about vision boards. "Your brain will work tirelessly to achieve the statements you give your subconscious mind. And when those statements are the affirmations and images of your goals, you are destined to achieve them."

I suggest you create a vision board with pictures and quotes about your future life. This can be on an app or physically cut out and placed on paper. The images and words should be from each part of your future good life—health, wealth, and love. You will automatically feel happier just by putting specific items on your board, and this will help focus your thinking and how you feel about the day—it's a great tool.

You can look at your board each morning and experience the feeling of having the item you see on the board. Your board should have a section of items that you desire to bring into your life, and each time an item comes to fruition, circle it or move it to the bottom of the board.

Start by feeling what it's like to allow those things to come to be. For instance, how will it feel to have that new watch you desire? Feel it like it already has manifested—that feeling has to come first. Think of there being two of you: one without the watch you want and one with that watch on your wrist. You are not just attracting that watch. You are creating that version of yourself, wearing the watch. The goal is to live the rest of your day as that person you have created with a new, high-end watch. Be that new you. Each day, you get to choose the version of yourself that you want to be.

8. Meditation (fifteen to twenty minutes)

Dr. Deepak Chopra posted on his website that new research shows that meditation restores the brain. A landmark study conducted by Massachusetts General Hospital found that as few as eight weeks of meditation helped people feel calmer and produced changes in various areas of the brain, including growth in the areas associated with memory, empathy, sense of self, and stress regulation. Dr. Wayne Dyer said in his book *The*

Power of Intention (2005), "What we think determines what happens to us, so if we want to change your lives, we need to stretch our minds."

Once we have set the tone for the day (by following the ideas in steps 1–7), we can quiet our minds and receive thoughts and inspirational actions for the day. When there is output, there must be input as well. We may spend most of the day talking but never taking the time to listen.

You only need to meditate for about fifteen minutes. Find a comfortable place, and close your eyes. Find or make some noise on which to focus. (You might listen to a fan or air conditioning.) Breathe in and out, and as each thought comes into your mind, let it go. Just let go of any and all thoughts you have; save them for later. You may only have one to three minutes of pure meditation, and that's okay. The more you do this, day after day, the greater benefit you will get from it. Practice makes perfect.

9. Exercise (eight minutes)

It's very important to make exercise part of your morning routine; get your body moving and your blood flowing. I like to do bigger workouts after work, but I never skip my morning eight-minute routine. You can go to my website for examples at www.fixyourstupid.com/exercise, but here's what I do for eight minutes:

- One minute doing plank
- One hundred crunches
- Twenty push-ups
- Twenty squats
- Ten jumping pull-ups

The entire nine steps of the thirty-day plan take less than an hour, and I promise it will exponentially boost your productivity. You will get much more done in less time. This thirty-day plan is just part of your journey in life. Enjoy the daily routines.

> There is a very real purpose to this plan. How you start your day is often how your start your life.
>
> —Louise Hay

You are creating new beliefs about what is possible and what you can create; about what you deserve. When you stick to something and consistently achieve even small things, you will change how you feel about what you deserve. This thirty-day (or longer) program is about your stopping the habit of living in reaction and taking control of your life and the direction of what tomorrow may bring. Dedicate yourself to the process, and forgive yourself if you falter. You will; I did. If you don't quit, the results can be amazing.

By doing the thirty-day plan, you will

- feel better and be in more control of your life;
- be more satisfied and happier, knowing that what you want is coming; and
- look back and see proof that you are smarter and that your life is now working better.

Always remember that you are moving forward to a life of attraction, so be committed to and focused on what you want. I also recommend that you keep your plan to yourself or tell as few people as possible until you see proof that it's working.

This will prevent anyone from judging you or slowing down your progress. Your only goal for the next thirty days is to feel better and feel better about yourself. You are right where you are supposed to be, and you cannot get it wrong.

1. How do I separate myself from who I want to be and what I want to have?

   _____

   _____

   _____

2. What is or has been my excuse or feeling that holds me back from becoming the best version of myself?

   _____

   _____

   _____

3. What am I willing to do to become that better version of myself?

   _____

   _____

   _____

4. Affirmations and Visualizations

Today I am creating and attracting a wonderful new day by appreciating everything in abundance.
Today I accept and appreciate my power to create abundance in my life.
Today, feeling good is enough.

CHAPTER 10

Learn to Be Excited about your stupid
(Because Now you know It Will Only Make you smarter)

Being entirely honest with oneself is a good exercise.

—Sigmund Freud

NOW THAT YOU'VE LEARNED WHAT YOUR STUPID IS AND HOW to change it to smart in any situation, it's time to make a choice. Are you okay with the fact that, at times and at some level, you will think and act stupidly again? I had to learn this lesson through many trials and tribulations. I have found there is never an end to your journey in your life or a point when you totally stop being stupid. You could reread this book in a few months or a year, and an entirely new reality could come from it.

As you grow, so does your understanding and reference point. I'm not saying you are unintelligent or uneducated.

Actually, it's the opposite. The bottom line is this: Are you willing to accept that stupid part of you when it shows up? Are you willing to view stupid thoughts or actions as opportunities to grow and discover more about yourself? No matter how smart you can be on a daily basis, are you willing to accept that old patterns remain that will take you to the stupid zone from time to time?

And can you be excited about that because it means you're growing?

If you said yes, keep moving forward by taking a big leap, by not judging but forgiving the stupid parts of yourself. Each time you feel stupid is an opportunity to become a better version of yourself or your dream self. You are never starting over because you are always starting from a new reference point with momentum and practice.

What Stupid Things Have You Done Lately?

Right now, tune in and ask yourself what stupid things you have done recently and most likely will do again at some point. Think about the many examples of stupid things you have done in your life and that you kept repeating. Accepting and forgiving the stupid part of you that surfaces at times allows you to move past it and keep moving forward toward your goals. This removes the resistance, or things that stop you from moving forward.

The key lesson I learned is that I cannot push or force things out of my life. I can only attract what I desire to me, and by doing this, I replace what I don't want by allowing in only the things that I do want. This process starts with changing my feelings.

The more you try to avoid a stupid action or thought and focus your attention on doing that, the more it will remain in your life. Once you accept the stupid, however, and forgive yourself for having that thought or taking that action, you can let that go—physically, emotionally, and mentally—and focus instead on what you truly want. It's as simple as changing the way you view and feel about the stupid part of you. I see my stupid self as being as much a part of me as my smart self, so I accept it. I will never give up on my stupid self. In fact, I will never give up on any part of me.

I've discovered that the stupid and smart parts of me teach me new ideas and bring me new situations and experiences. Knowing there is a good life that I deserve was my first step in the right direction. I wanted a better, healthy life; more wealth; and happier relationships. My being awake to my desires and the resulting situations and experiences can be very beneficial, even if they come through contrast. I believe all ideas come to me from whatever my current experience is, whether I like it or not. They just keep coming, and the key is for me to listen, not go to sleep or ignore them. I may have just accomplished something I have been working to attract, like a house, job, or relationship. Once I receive it, however, a new desire may appear that I want to manifest.

I recommend that you focus on the *process* most of all—the creating, not the actual creations. That way, you never have to get rid of your stupid or work on avoiding it; instead, focus on getting smarter about accomplishing the desires or goals you seek.

When I do that, I naturally let go—with no struggle—of the stupid parts of me and move to the next level of creativity in my life. It's a never-ending cycle of stupid/smart/stupid/smart and so on. We are complex beings, so getting comfortable with the fact that we will sometimes be stupid and at other times be smarter is imperative. That's the process by which we, as humans, operate.

A theme that runs through this book is that the entire universe is conspiring to give you everything you desire. In this chapter, you will know how much I believe in your ability to get what you want.

You Live in a Universe That Is Ever-Expanding, Never Static

Just as grass keeps growing, your thoughts grow too. Once you have a thought, it keeps changing. Think of how the young folks in Silicon Valley took the idea of computers and changed them from bulky things to something you carry in your hand. The reason is that the universe and *you* always are expanding.

In 1929, American astronomer Edwin Hubble demonstrated that the universe is expanding. Many consider his finding as one of the most important cosmological discoveries ever made; he formulated what is now known as Hubble's law.

To me, this means that if the universe is ever expanding in many dimensions, then our thoughts and wants and desires are expanding too. If we never wanted for anything more, then the universe would stop expanding. You just happen to be the center of the universe that revolves around you, and therefore, you interact with others who are doing the same thing. Ultimately, each of us has the power to control our destinies. The universe expands to transform itself to give us what we want, first through our thoughts and then through our inspired actions.

Life gets better and better as long as you find the feeling of the new and improved you. When you feel bad or have a negative emotion, it is because you asked the universe for direction to what you want. The universe answered, but you may not be following the directions you get. Then your stupid self makes you feel bad. It is like setting the GPS in your car; if you don't follow what it says to do, it will keep correcting you and trying to show you the way. As a result of your not listening, you will feel more and more negative, get lost, and keep traveling the wrong way. Boy, we humans can be stubborn at times.

This Is Where a Little Thinking Comes into Play

Remember to focus on the actual creation coming to fruition to excite and motivate yourself. Many of us don't take the time to think. You might say to yourself, "But I am *always* thinking." That may be true, but you don't always use smart or focused thinking. Taking the time to think is about preventing your reactive, stupid self from taking over and letting your smart, action-oriented self feel and act. Each creation that is manifested is a springboard to feeling even better and creating bigger manifestations; this is an important lesson to understand. Your stupid and smart follow the same principles. The stronger one gets, the stronger it gets; equally, the weaker one gets, the weaker it gets. This is known as momentum.

The *Merriam-Webster Dictionary* defines *momentum* as "a strength or force gained by motion or by a series of events." As you become smarter, you also will build momentum.

When I had several doctors working for me, we all started to see more and more patients. As a result, it sometimes took thirty to ninety days to get the billing done and money coming in. I had to remind my stupid mind, however, that the work I was putting in would make a positive impact on my finances.

Taking action and setting goals built a momentum, and my smart mind reminded me that in order to grow, I had to be patient and trust the process.

Imagine that your car is traveling at five miles an hour, and you run it into a tree. No problem, right? But that same car at one hundred miles an hour will cause big damage to you, your car, and the tree. When something expands or moves faster, it has more momentum and will become harder to stop.

Your life desires, your feelings, and your actions are all based upon the momentum you build. When you live without or lose focus, your momentum is often reactionary and takes you in a negative direction.

My goal in this final chapter is for you to realize that your momentum can be different in each one of your life areas: love, health, and wealth. I encourage you to use what you learned in this book about your inner guidance systems and your thinking choices. Remember you are in control, and when you focus on what you want, you will clearly see clues that will lead you there.

Read Below; Then Close Your Eyes and Picture Your Life Now

How do you want your life to be? How do you want your health to be? What kind of relationships do you want in your life? How much money do you want to have in your life? Close your eyes, and see what you see. Now decide on what you want, and focus on how it feels. Then listen to your inner self and follow the guidance you receive. These steps work!

Remember to appreciate what you have. Focus on what you have, and be happy; then you are focusing on what you have and what is coming, and you will get more of the same. I call this the "smart cycle." When asked what we want, most of us will say what we *don't* want and why. This is why I say to appreciate what you have and where you are on your journey right now; then feel any desire you have for what you want.

Remember that the universe hears you and provides everything you want. When you say, "I do not want to be poor," the universe sees you thinking *poor* and gives you more of that. When you say, "I want more money," and you feel abundant, the universe will take you in that direction. This is the way it works in 100 percent of your life, 100 percent of the time, and in 100 percent of every situation.

When I decided that I was feeling and looking unhealthy, I decided how I wanted to feel. All I did was hold on to that feeling! Within a few days, I noticed that my conversations with others were about being healthier. Days later, at a seminar in Phoenix, Arizona, my friend told me about a workout he had been doing. I asked him to talk to his trainer to see if there was someone I could hire in Ohio. And guess what? There was a gym like his just down the street from my office.

The better things get, the better they get, and the same is true of the opposite. The worse things get, the worse things get. This is only true because as things get bigger, you notice them more and expect those things to keep happening. The questions that remain are these: What do you want, and what are you willing to do to make it or allow it to happen?

Answer These Key Questions

Are you willing to be happy?

Are you willing to pay attention to how you feel and what you are thinking about those feelings?

If you said yes, then you have reaped the benefits that I wanted you to receive from this book. To get even clearer—to see how much you've learned and how you've changed your thinking since reading this book—take the same assessment test (below) that you took in chapter 1. This will show you how much you got from this book and how quickly you can change from stupid to smart.

Fix-Your-Stupid Assessment Test

Remember as you retake this test that true happiness is the balance or culmination of three key areas of your life—health, wealth, and love. You can be smarter in one or more of these areas.

Read each statement and reflect upon it. Score each question with a number, 1 through 10, with 1 being "never" and 10 being "always."

1. I take responsibility for everything that happens in my life, the good and the bad.
2. When I desire something, I focus more on what it's like to have it instead of the absence of it.
3. When I feel an impulse, I act on it quickly.
4. I bring whatever I desire and speak about into my life.
5. I generally look at the positive in every situation.
6. I practice a morning routine that sets the tone for my day.
7. I remember to first take care of myself so that I can inspire and give more to others.
8. I listen to my feelings to guide me in the direction I want to go.

9. I remember that when I want something, it is really not the physical thing I want but the feeling of having it.
10. I take the time to feel what it would be like to already have what I want.

Find your score and free gifts here: www.fixyourstupid.com/assessment.

What did you notice from assessing yourself now, as compared to when you took the test the first time? How did it make you feel? What actions will you take now?

Look at How Far You've Come!

Everyone fixes their stupid from where they are now. With consistent practice, you will slowly see a shift—a change; I promise. Each choice you make will teach you something different and unique. You cannot get it wrong, unless you just don't try. Allow yourself to grow and change.

When fixing your stupid, it is important to focus on how far you have come and where you are going. When driving your car, think of the time you spend looking in the rearview mirror compared to the time you spend looking ahead. Stay excited and motivated for where you are going.

Remember that even when you get there, you will have desires to continue to other places and to set other goals. There is a balance to fixing your stupid. Remember step 2 of the thirty-day plan: every morning, wake up and be thankful for another day to get smarter.

Take a moment to reflect and be thankful for all the good things that have happened to you since you've read this book. Think about anything good that occurred yesterday. It may be something big or something small. It is important to understand that you are always getting ready to be ready, to be ready, to be ready. Every day, each accomplishment is just another step in your day. It wasn't one huge leap that landed you where you are now, and where you are is not where you are stopping. Life is fluid and constantly changing, and you just need to adapt. Appreciate each accomplishment; it's getting you ready for more manifestation. Part of the fun in life is fixing your stupid. Life is abundant, and each day, each moment in time, is an opportunity to make a new, smarter decision. Since there are no mistakes and no ways to get it wrong, you are always moving in the right direction.

Blessings on your journey, my friend. I would love to hear about your experience. Feel free to share with me at info@fixyourstupid.com.

From stupid to smart,
Dr. Carl Rafey

1. Affirmations and Visualizations

I live my life on a want-to / choose-to basis.
What I focus on expands.
I am happy, I am healthy, I am wealthy, and I am ready.

RESOURCES

The following resources will help you on your way to fix your stupid:

- www.fixyourstupid.com—a website to complement this book and take you farther in your journey
- www.wholebodyintelligence.com—Steve   Sisgold's whole-body approach, which is mentioned in this book and offers a free BQ (Body Quotient) assessment
- www.alignedperfomanceinstitute.com—will help you make the most of your life
- www.mochihchu.com—Dr. Fred Schofield's website to teach energy management for chiropractors

For over twenty years, author, speaker, and coach Dr. Carl Rafey has been dedicated to helping people overcome their limitations. Dr. Rafey has shared the principles and methods in this book in multiple seminars for chiropractors, attorneys, and other health professionals. He also walks his talk by applying what he teaches in his own business career.

Dr. Rafey has built one of the most successful chiropractic businesses, at one point with multiple offices and several doctors whom he has personally trained to fix their stupid and enjoy megasuccess. He is the father of five children.

It's about time someone called out how stupid we humans can be. *Fix Your Stupid* is a spectacular read and a self-discovery course that will face out on my bookshelf, to remind me that I always have the choice to focus my thoughts and actions and, therefore, as the book teaches, create my own universe.

—Steve Sisgold, author of *What's Your Body Telling You?* and *Whole Body Intelligence*

In training thousands of chiropractors, I always teach that success doesn't come to you; you go to it. That's exactly what Dr. Carl Rafey has achieved by writing this very special book. The wisdom he shares will inspire and show you how to go toward and achieve the love, happiness, and relationships you desire and deserve. Charge ahead, and fix your stupid today. You'll be happy you did.

—Dr. Fred Schofield, Schofield Chiropractic Training